WALK-ON THIS WAY

WALK-ON THIS WAY

The On-Going Legacy of the Wisconsin Football Walk-On Tradition

BY
Joel Nellis &
Jake Kocorowski

This book is available in quantity at special discounts for your group or organization. For further information, contact:

KCI SPORTS PUBLISHING

3340 Whiting Avenue, Suite 5
Stevens Point, WI 54481
(800) 697-3756
Fax: (715) 344-2668

Cover Design: Emma Kumer
Book Layout and Design: Nicky Brillowski

Photos courtesy of *Wisconsin State Journal,* Associated Press and University of Wisconsin Athletic Department

Printed in the United States

DEDICATION

From Joel:

Jennifer – For always being by my side to support my dreams and goals. Thank you for encouraging me to begin this process and providing the support to see it through.

Adrik, Annika & Anden – I hope you embrace the walk-on mentality of pursuing your dreams without any guarantees, just the commitment you make to yourself to do your personal best.

Mara – You set a standard of excellence in our family that I always wanted to aspire to. Thanks for setting the bar high.

Paul Kollberg – Whose love of family and Badger athletics continues to live on in all of us.

Mom and Dad – Thank you for being my role models, teaching me the foundations of faith, success principals and giving me every opportunity to pursue my dreams. I'll never be able to truly thank you for how much you mean to me.

From Jake:

To Laura – For your unconditional love through all my hobbies that fell through the cracks (pro wrestling, scriptwriting, etc.), and her support in the one that I hope to have found my niche in. You are my rock, my best friend, and an amazing woman.

To Eli, Logan and Sammy – You're my greatest accomplishments in life. Set your sights high, work hard, stay humble. You can achieve what you set your mind to.

To my nephews, Mason and Chase – Believe in yourselves, and anything's possible.

To Grandma Borowski – For instilling in me the work ethic and drive to finish something through, especially when scrubbing your floors and cutting the lawn as a teenager.

TABLE OF CONTENTS

Dedication v

Acknowledgements vii

Foreword - Jim Leonhard 11

Chapter 1: What Makes a Walk-On? 15

Chapter 2: The Glue in the Foundation 24

Chapter 3: Rebuilding the Road to Pasadena . . 50

Chapter 4: Back-to-Back! 66

Chapter 5: From Paying to Play to Getting Paid
UW Walk-Ons in the NFL 82

Chapter 6: Faith, Football and Playing
For an Audience of One 127

Chapter 7: Breaking Through 154

Chapter 8: Embracing the Opportunity 172

Chapter 9: The Unheralded and Outcast –
The Specialists 190

Chapter 10: The Time to Shine 206

Chapter 11: Next Man Up 218

Chapter 12: The Legacy Comes Full Circle . . . 244

ACKNOWLEDGEMENTS

There are many people we'd like to thank for their time and contributions on this project. It all started after Jake wrote a long form article on the walk-on tradition for Bucky's 5th Quarter back in Deccember 2013. Joel approached Jake about working on a book in early 2014, and, with the blessing of their amazing wives, Jennifer and Laura, their journey began (well, after a certain co-author was able to get sleep after the birth of twin boys).

In June 2015, the project started with an interview with Marcus "Mookie" Trotter, and in one year, over 100 interviews have taken place between various players, coaches and media. We'd like to jointly thank all those who gave their time to speak with us for Walk-On This Way as interview subjects. The minutes (and sometimes hours) you spent with us were invaluable towards making the book a reality. These stories are timeless, and we hope they were properly represented when writing the book.

We would also like to thank those who offered advice in how we should go about writing the book. Thank you to Rob Reischel and Patrick Herb – the first two we spoke with regarding the long process – as well as Matt Lepay, Andy Baggot, Aaron Swerdlow, Sarah Streed, Jesse Temple, Dave Revsine and Mike Lucas. If we missed anyone, we deeply apologize, but thank you so much for helping us through the project.

We couldn't have written this without the assistance of the Wisconsin athletic department. Brian Lucas, Brian Mason, Chris McIntosh, Andrew Marlatt, Linda Wilkins, and

Lisa Powell all gave substantial time in answering our questions, setting up interviews and dealing with our consistent badgering (pun intended) for information.

Certain NFL teams and their amazing communications staffs helped us out in acquiring interviews, transcripts and information. Thank you to Tom Valente and the Baltimore Ravens, Scott Berchtold and the Buffalo Bills, Ted Crews and the Kansas City Chiefs, and both Amy Palcic and Omar Majzoub from the Houston Texans for all of their assistance.

Special thanks goes out to the following people who took some extra time to look at our work and provide feedback when needed right before we submitted this to the publisher. They include Chris Hein, Bobby Adamov, Eric Mahlik, Matt Katula, Luke Swan, Ethan Hemer, Ethan Armstrong, Zach Hampton, Paul Standring, Josh Hunt, Ben Worgull and Jason Galloway.

To Peter at KCI Sports Publishing, you took a chance on us with our extremely rough draft chapters for a manuscript that wasn't yet finished. Thank you for seeing the vision of the book and allowing us to capture these stories in print.

Joel would like to specifically thank those that made the walk-on journey as a football player for the Badgers possible. To Coach Kurt, Coach Verdin, Coach Schoessow and Coach Kope and all of the assistants for the Spartan Youth Program and Madison Memorial who helped provide me with a memorable youth and high school football experience.

I'll be forever thankful to Coach John Palermo for offering me the opportunity to walk-on at Wisconsin. Thanks to my position coaches, Tim Davis, Rob Ianello, and most importantly, Paul Chryst for helping me learn and improve at the tight end position. The offensive assistant coaches, most notably Coach Jim Hueber, who instilled a commitment to playing football the right way with an attention to detail and an unapologetic physicality. Thanks to Coach Brian Murphy who gave me the opportunity to contribute on special teams as a senior and for Coach Barry Alvarez for awarding me a scholarship for my last two seasons.

I couldn't ask for better teammates. A special thanks goes out to the tight end group for making meetings, practice and travel so enjoyable and full of endless memories. Lastly, to the roommates & teammates who've turned into my best friends - Jimmy, Owen, Jason, Brian, Matt & Sean - I appreciate you all more than you'll ever know.

I would also like to thank Jake for his tireless commitment and attention to detail on this project. He left no stone unturned in the process, diligently researching and rechecking every story and fact in this book.

Jake would like to first thank Joel for reaching out after his long form was initially published to talk about this project. Nearly three years after publishing the initial article on Bucky's 5th Quarter, I never thought I'd take on an all-encompassing look at a group of players I admired since I was a kid. Through our consistent communication during the project, whether interview planning or organizing our thoughts on the screen, you've become a great friend, and I hope for that to continue for years to come. Thanks for taking a chance on me.

A special thanks to the site manager of Bucky's 5th Quarter, Mike Fiammetta, for allowing me to explore the walk-on tradition at Wisconsin with that long form article. If it wasn't for his blessing, who knows if this idea grows into the book that it is. His consistent mentoring and guidance helped me improve as a writer substantially, and his willingness to bring on our podcast opened the gates to become the writer and now author that I am (still feels weird to say, to be honest).

I'm not even in this "media" game unless my old independent wrestling promoter/brother and former ESPN Milwaukee radio personality, "The Polish Rifle" Scott Wisniewski, agrees to start doing an independent sports podcast in the summer of 2012. Since 2013 when we joined B5Q, the Kielbasa Kings Sports Extravaganza has recorded hundreds of thousands of listens. He honed my voice and taught me the ins and outs of sports talk. I appreciate every discussion and debate we've had. I'm forever grateful.

And special thanks to my family, who fed my keen interest in sports at an early age with a comprehensive encyclopedia of all Green Bay Packers statistics in the third grade, to my best friends (Aaron, Adam and Phil) and others. I appreciate all of your support through the years.

FOREWORD
BY JIM LEONHARD

Jim Leonhard was one of the most successful players to ever patrol the Badgers defensive backfield. The product of tiny Tony, Wisconsin, arrived on campus in 2001 as an unheralded, 5-foot-8 walk-on and left four years later as a three-time first-team All-American. Leonhard played in every game of his four-year career, including each of the last 39 as a starting safety, en route to becoming one of the best defensive players in school history. He matched UW's school record with 21 interceptions in his career, the fourth-most in Big Ten history, and finished with 50 passes defended. He is also the school's all-time leader in single-season and career punt return yardage. Leonhard would go on to enjoy a 10-year career in the NFL. He was inducted into the Wisconsin Athletic Hall of Fame in 2015.

"Mike Broussard, get the HELL out! Jimmy Leonhard, get in!"

Those words from secondary coach Ron Cooper during a practice in August of 2002 greatly changed the trajectory of my college football career and, ultimately, my life.

What happened that day wasn't an unusual event: players get yelled at and replaced all the time in practice. Personnel changes may not last more than a couple of reps or at most one practice; in most circumstances, the player will return to his original spot in the rotation.

But I remember after practice that day, sitting back and thinking maybe this is it? Maybe this is the opportunity that I can run with.

As it turns out, it was. Coach Cooper putting me in at strong safety that day set me on a path that would allow me to make 39 career starts at Wisconsin and go on to play 10 years in the National Football League.

As a walk-on, all I was looking for was an opportunity. I was an undersized, lightly recruited, option-quarterback coming out of Flambeau High School in northwestern Wisconsin when I decided to walk-on at UW. Contributing on special teams as a true freshman gave me the confidence and experience I needed to expand my role heading into the following season.

Being looked at as the under-sized, overachiever always frustrated me. It really did. It motivated me to go out there again and again to prove that not only did I belong, but that you could count on me to win. It was a mistake in recruiting to not give me a scholarship. That's how I always felt about it.

Oddly enough my basketball skills may have played a part in me getting noticed by the coaching staff.

During conditioning drills early in 2002, I got the chance to showcase some of my athleticism. The coaching staff would often find ways to break up the monotony of practice with competitions involving different sports. On this particular day a basketball dunk contest was scheduled. I'm only 5-foot-8, but I was all in. The coaches were looking at me like, 'What is this guy doing in a dunk contest?' Luckily, I had played basketball with a handful of the guys, so they knew I could play, and they knew I could jump. I could barely palm the ball, so when I dunked I had to dunk hard. That's a good thing in a dunk contest. I was able to throw a couple down and got the victory over John Stocco and Jonathan Welsh much to the surprise of the coaching staff.

It might seem silly to think a dunk contest would have anything to do with my football career, but at that moment, it helped get me noticed.

Fast forward to that August, and I'm in a packed Camp

Randall Stadium about to make my first career start against Fresno State. You always remember your first career start. There were some nerves, but I was confident and ready. I was able to grab two interceptions that day as we hung on for a tough 23-21 victory. At a certain point it gets down to focusing on the game plan and going out and doing what I've always tried to do – make plays.

I consider it an honor to be included as part of the great tradition of walk-ons at Wisconsin. Now that I am coaching at UW, I am routinely reminded of, and inspired by, the commitment and determination of our walk-on players.

In the following pages, I hope Badger fans will enjoy looking back at the contributions these players have made to the success of Wisconsin football. I'm confident there will be many more successful walk-on stories to add in the years to come.

CHAPTER ONE

What Makes A Walk-On?

Walk-ons aren't uncommon in college football. Coaching staffs have to replenish talent each season with players who would "walk on" to the program and pay for their own college education while balancing both athletics and academics.

What's not common is the level of impact and success walk-ons have had on Wisconsin football since Barry Alvarez arrived in Madison over 26 years ago.

Upon his arrival from Notre Dame in 1990, Alvarez set about to drastically change the fortunes of Wisconsin football for years to come.

First, he built a wall around Wisconsin's borders to keep those talented in-state recruits from leaving for Iowa, Michigan and Notre Dame. Second, he implemented a physical, run-oriented scheme that would become the calling card of UW's offense. Lastly, he would mimic what his former head coach, Bob Devaney, mastered in his time in Lincoln with Nebraska's walk-on program.

Those tenets would be sown into the fabric of Wisconsin football. A program mired in abysmal futility during the late 1980s, compiling a 6-27 record under Don Morton from 1987-89, would be resurrected and produce a conference and Rose Bowl Championship team in just four seasons.

"They are my erasers. That's how I labeled them," acknowledged Alvarez, referring to UW's walk-ons. "They were the difference maker. They were the edge in our program. Every coach looks for an edge. I don't care what it is, there are a lot of different things. If you grow up in Florida or Georgia, your edge is your skill players. At Wisconsin, we're going to have big guys and we're going to have additional guys through our walk-on program. They're the edge that we had. They gave us the edge when you had limited scholarships. We gave respect to the walk-ons knowing that we would get a handful or more every year that would end up playing for us."

Sometimes those highly-regarded recruits a program signs may not pan out. There could be a variety of reasons, from unfortunate injuries throughout their career to discipline issues. Some of the scholarship players just don't live up to the hype they gain in their prep careers. Wisconsin's successfully recruited the walk-ons to not just be scout team bodies or special teams players. They've become those "erasers" as Alvarez mentioned, performing when called upon, but also consistently playing their way into contributing roles on both sides of the ball.

Simply put, walk-ons – those described as "undersized, underdeveloped and under-recruited" by former head coach Bret Bielema – have made a vital and significant impact on the success of the Wisconsin program in the past 25 seasons.

"I say year in and year out, consistently, Wisconsin seems to me to have – certainly in the Big Ten – the best walk-on tradition," said Big Ten Network studio host Dave Revsine. "While I'm more familiar with the Big Ten in the last decade or so than I am with any other conference because I follow it most closely, it seems to me that in terms of getting consistent production from walk-ons in key positions, I can't imagine there's anyone that's getting more out of their walk-on program than Wisconsin."

From a national perspective, there's always the great walk-on stories you see on ESPN College Gameday of the one player who overcame the odds to make an impact on his team, the one player who personified perseverance that gets that long-awaited scholarship.

"Often times these are not the kids who were anointed in

high school as the next best thing so they had to fight and scrap. They had different memories and landmark moments in their football careers, and I just found that really appealing," *Sports Illustrated's* Lindsay Schnell said, who extensively writes about walk-ons at a national level.

Only a few programs have cultivated a culture of walk-ons contributing each season. Most schools will add a handful of walk-ons for depth during training camp so they have bodies to scrimmage the starters. Others may rely upon them in times of sanctions against their respective programs, but few Division I teams truly embrace the tradition of walk-ons.

"Kansas State, Nebraska, and Wisconsin are the three that come to my mind that it is celebrated," Schnell elaborated. "It is sort of a badge of honor if you're a walk-on, especially if you're a walk-on who earns a scholarship. And I think because it has been proven that it works at those places, that they will give you a fair shot, it's not as scary to walk on there."

Wisconsin natives Joe Panos, Sam Veit, Chris Hein and Chad Cascadden were walk-ons who contributed heavily to the Badgers' first Rose Bowl championship team during the 1993 season. Their success served as the blueprint for walk-on starters Jason Doering, Donnel Thompson, Bob Adamov and Mark Tauscher during the 1998 and 1999 seasons when UW won back-to-back Rose Bowls.

Dozens of others, including Jim Leonhard and Chris Maragos, have continued that walk-on success from the early-to-late 2000s. As of summer 2016, 90 walk-ons have earned scholarships since 1990 when Alvarez took over the football program. Each of the six Rose Bowl teams the Badgers have fielded since 1993 had at least two or more starters walk on to the program. Some of those years had at least four walk-ons start in certain stretches of the season. In all but one season a walk-on was named as a team captain.

Many walk-ons have etched their names in Wisconsin history through the years. Wide receiver Jared Abbrederis is tied with Brandon Williams as the program's all-time receptions leader with 202 catches, while also owning the single-season mark with 78. Quarterback Joel Stave became Wisconsin's all-time leader for wins as a starter (31). Heading into the 2016 season, eleven walk-ons have played in 50 career games.

"Nebraska has an incredible tradition of walk-on success," Revsine said. "That would be one program nationally you kind of have to look at to be in the conversation with Wisconsin, but what's amazing about Wisconsin is their walk-ons are not just for depth. They've turned out to be some of their star players through the years and guys who've gone on to make huge contributions, not just at the college level but the pro level."

But where do they come from?

Many walk-ons are in-state products who turn down what some may deem as lesser scholarship offers for the chance to play in Madison. Current-day Football Championship Subdivision (FCS) schools like Illinois State, Northern Iowa and powerhouse North Dakota State, pursued these young men and offered a complete or partial scholarship. Division II and Division III schools, particularly within Minnesota and Wisconsin, could offer opportunities to play right away.

Even with those options, many felt a chance to compete in the Big Ten was just too much to pass up.

"I had decided that the smaller schools like Illinois State, Northern Iowa, all those would be there if it didn't work out at Wisconsin," former defensive lineman Ethan Hemer said. "I very badly wanted to be a part of the state school and represent my hometown on the biggest stage. I had grown up watching the Rose Bowl teams and seeing all these great players and the success that Wisconsin had started to build. I wanted to be a part of that. It was too big of an opportunity to turn down, so I decided to go to Madison."

Some may seem to come out of nowhere, or were under-recruited for a reason. Why? They matured later in their teenage years, like Doering or J.J. Watt. Alvarez and Notre Dame head coach Lou Holtz referred to those kids as late bloomers.

"We all knew guys that were in seventh grade and had

mustaches and beards. They would have a six o'clock shadow by the time the school day ended. They're bigger than everybody," Alvarez explained. "Then by their senior year in high school, they're four inches shorter than everyone else.

"We have a state with a number of late bloomers – kids who haven't quite yet grown into their frames. In recruiting there were a few things we'd always look at. We would check their wrists, look how big their feet are, look how big their shin bone is, check their shoulders, look at the size of their mother – we'd do all that stuff. That's what we looked at. Mike Verstegen was probably 230 pounds when he came to Wisconsin. He ends up being the starting tackle on the 1994 Rose Bowl team, and a third-round NFL pick. He was 6-foot-6, 290 pounds. He was a classic late bloomer. Raw, big boned. You knew he was going to grow. He came in as an outside linebacker. We looked at him and said, 'No, you're going to be a tackle.'"

"Lou and I used to talk about that. We all knew guys who matured early. The late bloomers took some projection during recruiting, but they had a chance to help you."

Another defining characteristic of these walk-ons involves their competitive drive bleeding into multiple sports during their high school days. Leonhard was as an all-state honoree in football, basketball, and baseball. Doering almost went to a junior college in Illinois for baseball before coaches found him during the state's annual high school all-star game in the summer. Fullback Bradie Ewing punished opposing linebackers and defensive lineman on that special, high-powered offense in 2011. Before that, he was offered not just a preferred walk-on spot by Bielema and the football staff, but also by Bo Ryan and the men's basketball team at Wisconsin. The list of multi-sport prep players who would walk-on to UW goes on and on, and it's given them a distinct advantage in always being in shape, always training and always competing.

Some walk-ons came to UW with a chip on their shoulder, striving to prove people wrong or achieve what others thought they couldn't. Those in the media or outside looking in could perceive those players to be modern-day Rudy stories, who after years of being denied their place, overcame, persevered and had their personal triumph. In some instances, like Josh Hunt's 89-yard punt return against Western Michigan or Nate Tice's 17-yard touchdown run in 2010, this metaphor may ring true.

For Leonhard, Thompson, and Luke Swan and a host of others, they were simply overlooked. Some were hidden due to their geographical location (hailing from a small-town in rural Wisconsin) or injuries suffered during critical times in their high school careers.

"I was always the overachiever, the walk-on," Leonhard said, noting the frustration that moniker left him. "I felt like it kind of slighted what I had done. First of all, I was an All-American as a sophomore – that was not the path of Rudy at Notre Dame. He played a handful of snaps in his last game. To get that comparison brought up in every interview it felt like a slap in the face."

When they get on the field, players have to perform regardless of prep background or misguided talent evaluations. Scholarship kids may have the luxury of extended opportunities to prove their lead recruiter or position coach right in assessing their value to the program. Their reps in practice are normally higher than that of walk-ons, who only get one or two opportunities per series of plays to prove that they understand the schemes and concepts. Many acknowledge and are accepting of that fact.

"As a walk-on you have to prove yourself over and over again so the less mistakes you make, the more probable it is that you'll be sticking around with the team and more likely that they'll use you in the grand scheme of things," former receiver Paul Hubbard noted. "So you have that pressure on your shoulders as a walk-on, especially with a big-time Division I program"

"(Defensive coordinator) Dave Doeren told me several times, 'Hey you only get a handful of reps, especially starting off,'" linebacker Ethan Armstrong said. "'The guys we're bringing in on scholarship are going to get their shot first.

You're going to get your shot. I can't tell you when that's going to be, so you have to be ready for it.'"

When called upon, many have seized that shot to showcase their skills and make an impression. What makes Wisconsin football even more special is the fact many players don't know who's on scholarship and who's sending a check to the university each semester. Both scholarship and walk-on players are treated with the same demeanor and respect by the coaches inside Camp Randall Stadium and its training facilities. Some college locker rooms, like that at Arkansas prior to Bielema's arrival in 2012, weren't that fortunate.

The former Badgers head coach – himself a former walk-on at Iowa – has fashioned the Razorbacks' walk-on program in similar fashion to his former employers. According to Bielema, 15 walk-ons have received scholarships since he took over in Fayetteville.

On an emotional and existential level the walk-on experience at Wisconsin personifies the state's culture. They're a reflection of those 9-to-5, bring your lunch pail to work citizens who call the Badger State home.

"Wisconsin is a blue-collar state, and just having guys that might not get the recruiting attention they deserve but having that mentality that they're going to work no matter what happens," linebacker Marcus Trotter said back in 2013. "I mean that's what this program was built on. We always face teams that are perceived to be more athletic than us or better than us, but our hard work and dedication allows us to play with anyone in the country. That's our motivation."

"I think the walk-on program has done a lot more for Wisconsin football as a whole – pee wee level all the way up to college," said kicker Mike Allen, fifth all-time in school history with 41 field goals. "It gives kids an opportunity to dream. There's no doubt about it that there are hundreds, if not thousands, of kids that watched Jimmy Leonhard do what he did while he was in school. Knowing that he was a walk-on, knowing that he was this little, short guy that so many people overlooked, it provides hope and dreams for kids."

That inspiration for the thousands of young Badgers fans, from Superior to Pleasant Prairie, can also be drawn from those who went from no stars on the recruiting services to playing on Sundays. Eighteen former walk-ons have taken their success to the next level on NFL 53-man rosters. Four played for over a decade in the NFL, a couple were honored with Pro Bowl selections and some even won a Super Bowl.

Arguably the biggest name in football today is J.J. Watt, the Houston Texans' star defensive end. Many know the story of the Pewaukee native who held only two Division I Power Five conference offers from Minnesota and Colorado. He committed to Central Michigan as a tight end after a back and forth courtship with the Gophers, then left the Chippewas to walk-on at Wisconsin. After a position change and sitting out the 2008 season, he began to impose his will on the defensive line for his final two years in Madison.

His college success translated into an amazing five-year NFL career in which he has four All-Pro selections and was honored as the Associated Press NFL Defensive Player of the Year three times. The superstar now has his own logo courtesy of Reebok. His "Dream Big, Work Hard" motto and his charity, the Justin J. Watt Foundation, go hand-in-hand with the walk-on tradition he experienced at Wisconsin.

For every success story like Watt, Maragos and Leonhard, dozens of other walk-ons experience a different set of circumstances. The themes and journeys of each athlete may be similar, but each has his own individual story. Some like Tauscher or Trotter struggled to break into the two-deep on the Badgers' depth chart, but contributed later on in their careers as starters or on special teams. Others fill the gaps when needed in pressing game time situations.

The rest are those that might not ever see the field during game days, but often assist the team in preparing for each week's opponents as members of the scout team. Jeff Holzbauer, who Hubbard lovingly referred to as "Socrates," was known for his knowledge of the UW offense in the early-to-mid 2000s. As Leonhard notes, all of the walk-ons contributed to the "glue" that's elevated and kept Wisconsin football a successful program.

"There's been so many great walk-ons that have had the amazing numbers and careers," Leonhard said, "but you look past those and every single year there's another handful that graduate that really make up what the program is all about."

How much does Wisconsin value its walk-ons? The program has a wall in its locker room dedicated to those walk-ons who have earned letters and scholarships, along with those who have been voted captains and made it to the NFL. | Jake Kocorowski

CHAPTER TWO

The Glue in the Foundation

On New Year's Day 1994, three Wisconsin Badgers stood at midfield inside the Rose Bowl. Surrounded by 101,237 fans at the 80th rendition of the "Granddaddy of Them All," they looked across the 50-yard line to see four UCLA Bruins, led by quarterback Wayne Cook and safety Marvin Goodwin. In between both squads stood the referee and Star Trek's Captain Kirk.

It was the first bowl game for Wisconsin since the 1984 season, its first time in Pasadena since 1963. It would be a tough challenge facing a Pac-10 team boasting six first team All-Americans, including Goodwin, wide receiver J.J. Stokes and linebacker Jamir Miller.

During pre-game ceremonies, actor William Shatner shook hands with guard Joe Panos, nose guard Lamark Shackerford, and reserve fullback Jeff Wirth before he and the referee started the proceedings for the game's coin flip. Backing up starting fullback Mark Montgomery, Wirth was known for his contributions on special teams, earning UW's Special Teams Player of the Year award for his efforts during that 1993 season.

What stood out most as they faced their adversaries was the sea of red dominating the Bruins' home stadium. Wisconsin fans flocked in droves to the greater Los Angeles area to see their team compete for a Rose Bowl championship for the first time in over three decades.

What may not have been as noticeable was two of those three players in cardinal and white were walk-ons. If not for a late scholarship given to Shackerford before the 1990 season, all three UW representatives for that coin toss would have been walk-ons.

Emotions ran high for the captains at the 50-yard line that day.

"Honestly, it was a little overwhelming. It goes back to when I was a kid and I just loved Badger football. I grew up in Wisconsin, so the Rose Bowl was always a big deal," Wirth admitted. "We basically had three channels back then so when it came to the bowl season, the Rose Bowl was the game I watched."

The 1993 team would take the Wisconsin football program to new heights with their Rose Bowl victory in California, but the progression to greatness took four seasons under Alvarez. As the coaching staff worked to keep the highly-regarded in-state recruits within its borders, a significant number of walk-on contributors acted as the glue in filling out the roster in those early years of Alvarez' regime. Many would contribute on special teams, a few would see action as starters or key reserves and one would even ascend from a NCAA Division III defensive lineman to starting right tackle and team captain.

****

Wisconsin's downward descent into mediocrity accelerated during Don Morton's three seasons in Madison. The Badgers mustered only six wins from 1987-89, including a 3-21 conference record. For the players, it was a difficult time to be a part of Wisconsin football. According to former All-Big Ten defensive tackle Don Davey, many of his teammates wouldn't sport their team-issued apparel due to being embarrassed for the program.

"As a player, you want to believe you have good coaches in place, that you've got a good system in place, you've got good leadership from both the athletic director and the head coach in the program," said Davey, a scholarship player. "During that time, we kept telling ourselves that things will get better. In hindsight, in comparison between when Barry came in and when Morton came in, it was night and day. The Morton years were tough. We struggled on the football field. We were running an offense that literally had no success in the Big Ten. We had some good defensive teams, but we were always down early. The offense was always turning the ball over, putting us behind the eight ball. It was a rough stretch."

Alvarez was hired to turn things around starting with the 1990 season by new director of athletics Pat Richter – the former Wisconsin three-sport standout and All-American. With the newfound energy needed to jolt the athletic department out of its $2.1 million debt, and with the support of university chancellor Donna Shalala, the plans were in motion to resuscitate the program. Coming from Lou Holtz' Fighting Irish staff, the former Nebraska linebacker led a defense that contributed to a national championship in 1988. He also had that winning pedigree from his days as a player under Bob Devaney and as an assistant under Hayden Fry at Iowa.

In that introductory press conference, Alvarez famously (and boldly) declared that fans better buy their season tickets before they sell out. There was a promise of brighter days ahead after the dismal seasons under Morton.

"That spring when they became available, I bought season tickets, and I'm covering the team," said former WTMJ radio voice Brian Manthey, who called the 1994 Rose Bowl. "That's how persuasive he was. I had a sense that between Barry Alvarez, Pat Richter and Donna Shalala, that this was a different animal."

It would take three seasons to get to the promised land of Pasadena, though, and that whole different animal approach did not show in the won-loss column right away.

The Badgers stumbled to a 1-10 record that first year, but progress was evident. From the first team meeting after Christmas break, Alvarez asserted himself as the leader of the program and commanded respect. Under strength and conditioning coach Scott Reirdon and later John Dettman, team workouts would become more demanding and intense, with Davey recalling his teammates vomiting during the first day of conditioning. Spring ball became more aggressive as well, with full pads and contact forging the hard-nosed demeanor needed to play competitively in the Big Ten.

"The workouts were much more scientifically based and structured, which led to everyone getting an opportunity to grow to their potential," walk-on cornerback Korey Manley recalled. "But there was also a high degree of accountability. They set a standard, and whether it was in the classroom, on the field, or in the weight room – if you didn't meet it, you were dismissed."

It wasn't just the physical aspect of the game that the coaching staff meant to overhaul, they also got into the precise nuances of offensive and defensive schemes to put their players in a position to succeed. Davey recalled a practice where he, as a defensive tackle, was supposed to play a "shade" to the guard – or line up towards his opponent's outside shoulder pads. Before the play was even snapped, defensive coordinator and defensive line coach Dan McCarney blew the whistle and immediately disciplined the Academic All-Big Ten selection.

"He said, 'This is what a shade looks like. Right here!'" Davey said with a laugh. "I mean, that level of detail where linebackers had to be exactly four and a half yards deep, your shade is nine inches on the guard's shoulder pad, not six inches. Those type of things. That's ultimately why we were so successful. There's a science and a precision to football, and things needed to be done a certain way to give you the best advantage. We never had that level of detail before with the prior staff."

The new demands placed on the players by the coaches didn't come without some turnover on the roster. Those who couldn't cut the increased intensity would bolt from the program. Alvarez said around 52 Badgers would leave the program during the transition. It should be noted the roster numbers were larger and not subject to the same current day limit of 120 players.

The consistent shuffling of bodies in practice was noticeable to players and coaches alike, however.

"I think some of the players realized they couldn't play at this level," Alvarez noted. "I think some couldn't keep up. There were some discipline issues. They didn't like the tempo we kept, how we practiced, the out of season conditioning."

The team would improve its win total by four games in 1991 by going 5-6. UW started 3-0, but stumbled during conference play to the tune of six losses in eight games. They would finish the year on a high note, beating Minnesota on the road and Northwestern at home. Both wins were huge for the program as one ended a 19-game conference losing streak and the other a 23-game road losing streak.

****

There was a sprinkling of walk-ons contributing significantly that 1991 season. A player, whose birth name was Zois Panagiotopoulos, would end up playing and starting at two positions along the offensive line that year. You won't find that name in the UW record books, but he's known throughout Badger country as Joe Panos.

Panos walked on to Wisconsin after playing the 1989 season at Division III Wisconsin-Whitewater. He'd have to sit out the 1990 season due to NCAA transfer rules while acclimating to Division I, Big Ten football. With the weeding out of the weak in Alvarez' first campaign as head coach, opportunities opened up for the scout-team defensive lineman.

"He really was an undersized guy that came in playing defense, but he was a tough guy and you saw he had the want to," said Alvarez. "We had some holes in the offensive line and thought we would move him over there."

That season, Panos lined up as a starter for nine games, splitting time between center and right guard. He played 550 snaps, impressive for a kid who had mere weeks to learn the ins and outs of Wisconsin's offense between spring and summer camp. His greatest days in a Badgers uniform were still to come.

The '91 season also started the four-year reign of Sam Veit as starting punter. Veit, who still ranks fifth all-time in career punts (209), sixth in yards (8,016) and tenth all-time in yards per punt (38.4), wasn't supposed to be the punter. Alvarez and his coaching staff received a commitment from an Ohio prospect named Bobby Knapp, and he would earn the starting job for the Badgers as they headed into the 1991 season opener against Western Illinois.

Veit initially tried out to earn an invite to fall camp, with the help of academic-athletic consultant Jerome Fishbain. He solidified his spot as the second punter on the roster but would see the field sooner than he ever thought, as he was named the kickoff specialist in his first ever game. Kicker Rich Thompson was nursing an injury, which allowed Veit and Matt Krueger, a redshirt freshman walk-on from a suburb of Milwaukee, the chance to make an impact.

"Here I am, a freshman kicker, I think I was still 17 years old," Veit recalled with a chuckle, "kicking off the first game of Coach Alvarez's second season. I told everyone I knew, 'You better get to this game, because this might be the only time I ever get to play.'"

That wouldn't be the case. In the second quarter, Knapp couldn't handle a snap that resulted in the Leathernecks starting at UW's own 32-yard line. The short field led to a quick touchdown and a 13-0 deficit for the Badgers. The coaching staff pulled the Wadsworth, Ohio product and inserted the in-state kid to provide the stability of just getting the ball off. Veit would do just that, and though his first punt was only 30 yards, he would take over duties the rest of the year.

He averaged 35.9 yards per boot that season, and though he didn't put up spectacular numbers, he anchored the position.

"Sam Veit wasn't the tallest, wasn't the strongest leg, but, as Coach Alvarez would say, he never flinched," current

Buffalo head coach Lance Leipold said, a former Wisconsin graduate assistant from 1991-93. "He handled the job, he handled the snaps that maybe were erratic, and just kind of won the job and never looked back."

Knapp would leave the program the next year, leaving the Racine Case prospect as the team's choice at punter until his final season in 1994. Along the way, he earned second-team All-Big Ten honors as a sophomore in 1992 when he averaged 39.6 yards per punt. Only 19 of his 65 punts were returned. Off the field, he was an academic all-conference selection his final three seasons.

"I think Sammy was just a model of consistency," explained former scholarship guard Joe Rudolph, now Wisconsin's offensive coordinator and offensive line coach. "Sam was cool, calm and collected. You looked at him, and he wouldn't have much to say but you knew you could count on him and he would get it done in any given situation. You loved that and he always brought that to the table."

Rudolph noted the 1991 squad felt a energy around the program. They believed they could compete and win games, a feeling that was absent for many of the previous seasons. Five wins in a season was the most since 1985, and there was a confidence building within Camp Randall.

The Badgers beat its first ranked opponent since the 1985 season, defeating No. 12 Ohio State 20-16 in the fourth game of the year. Along with Veit's second-team all-conference honors, guard Chuck Belin, linebacker Gary Casper, nose guard Shackerford and kicker Thompson were awarded first-team All-Big Ten honors.

****

Korey Manley played in all 11 games as a redshirt freshman in 1990, then went on to become UW's Special Teams Player of the Year in 1991 (twelve former walk-ons from 1990 to 2016 have won that honor) while also serving as the fifth defensive back when the Badgers went to their nickel defense. The North Fond du Lac native downed six punts inside the five-yard line and was a leader on the kickoff and punt coverage units. In their 28-20 loss at Indiana in 1991, Wirth blocked a punt that Manley recovered in the end zone for a touchdown.

"You're talking about an undersized high school athlete, who was a running back and a defensive back, who was a point guard in basketball, who was a catcher in baseball, who was a sprinter in track," Wisconsin football and basketball analyst Mike Lucas recalled warmly. "You're talking about someone who was extremely smart, in the top two percent of his class. Athletically though, he came into question only because he was 5-foot-8, 150 pounds. That's what he was in high school, but he had the heart of a champion. The only scholarship offer Korey got was from the Reserve Officer Training Corp (ROTC), and that's how he got to the University of Wisconsin.

"While he was here that first year, he wasn't playing football. I remember he called the football office and asked about trying out because he missed the sport," Lucas continued. "It was during the Morton years, and they said they'd get back to him."

Manley never heard from the Morton staff. Wanting to explore his options to get on the team, Korey became impatient and enlisted the help of his high school coach Brian Harney. Harney, who

Korey Manley (24) attempts to block a punt during Big Ten play. | Wisconsin State Journal played linebacker at Wisconsin and lettered from 1971-73, intervened on his behalf to get Manley a tryout. The northeastern Wisconsin product, who by that time was up to 180 pounds, finally made the team.

Manley worked his way up the ranks of a group of walk-ons and scout team players called "The Pit Bulls." The rag tag group would be asked to mimic the team's opponents each week during the special teams period. Manley credits assistant Jay Norvell for developing each member's intense mentality when facing the starting coverage units. The tenacity and work ethic shown by these players would later define some of those special team units.

"Barry always really enjoyed his relationship with the walk-on players, and they were respected," Norvell said. "As a young coach, I learned that from him. I looked for guys that I felt had a burning desire to make an impact. A lot of those kids were walk-ons – they were trying to prove themselves. They had a great spirit for the game, and they were trying to prove that they deserved to be in a Division I program. I took that burning desire and I gave them a platform to show how badly they wanted to play. It really gave us an incredible chemistry because we had a handful of guys that were incredibly tough-minded and aggressive that really wanted to prove to everybody else that they belonged. They made an incredible impact."

"When Barry first gave me that job," Norvell continued, "he said, 'I want our special teams to be like a bunch of crazy Banshee Warriors.'"

Norvell would use motivation to get the group to that level.

Special team's awards were handed out each week to a certain player who performed well the previous game. The incentive wasn't just the recognition, but the position group coach of that particular player would be subject to some form of tomfoolery during team meetings. On the field, the former Iowa standout found ways to have some fun with his coverage and return units.

"For the special teams' guys, we'd take them on the field,"

Norvell recalled. "We'd scream at them and ask them if they were warriors. We gave out these warrior head stickers. If you remember the scene in *Full Metal Jacket* where the sergeant's screaming at the enrollee:

"'Are you a warrior?'

"'Sir yes sir!'

"'Well, let me see your war face!'

"They'd start screaming and showing their war face, and if theirs was good enough, we'd put eye black on them and they were part of 'The Pit Bulls.' It was really a badge of honor."

"He started the 'Pit Bulls,' and was just an amazing, fiery coach. He had a great attitude that really got you going," Manley said of Norvell. "That was really the moniker for the group because he just wanted to stir everyone up, get everybody excited like a pack of rabid dogs. He would encourage us to really set the tone for kickoffs and kickoff returns."

Manley was elevated to one of the starting cornerbacks in 1992, playing in all 11 games and contributing 84 tackles. He also contributed on special teams, blocking a punt against Indiana in a 10-3 loss. On top of that, he would lead the team in kickoff returns and yardage, averaging 24.3 yards per return. His play would earn him an AP honorable mention all-conference selection.

"I thought Korey really opened the door for many of the walk-ons who followed, whether it be a Joe Panos, Chad Cascadden, Vince Zullo, Chris Hein, Bob Adamov, Matt Davenport, Jason Doering – you can continue to go on and on and on," Lucas said. "Korey was one of those good early stories of someone getting an opportunity who was viewed by many, including Morton, of being too small and not good enough to play. Alvarez gave him a chance to prove himself in practice, and he just worked himself into the starting lineup."

****

UW started the 1992 season 3-1 but would lose five of

their next seven, including heartbreaking, one-point defeats at Iowa and versus Illinois at home. The Badgers could have had the opportunity to head to the Independence Bowl or the Freedom Bowl if they beat Northwestern in the last game of the season at Evanston. Unfortunately, a fumble in the last minute of the game cost the team a chance to attempt a field goal for the win. Two missed field goals and a botched punt block attempt could have swung the game in UW's direction and sealed a bowl berth as well.

"That wasn't the only heart breaker that year," Alvarez elaborated further, as four of the team's six losses that season were by one touchdown or less. "We lost a really tough one to Iowa on a bad call. We lost to Illinois on a bad call. They called a holding call when we had the game iced. Indiana, we caught a skinny post for a touchdown, and the receiver was barely out of bounds. So it was one of those deals where if we had those guys for more time, that's a 9-2 team, maybe 8-3. We found some ways not to win."

Heading into the 1993 season, the players realized this could be something special, and so did their leader. Walk-on Chris Hein, who earned one of the starting outside linebacker spots in the spring, recalled a meeting prior to the season at Holy Name Seminary, where the team practiced during the preseason. Three years' earlier in a similar team meeting in the same auditorium, offensive lineman Nick Polczinski famously pushed to have one of the team's goals be to go undefeated. He was ultimately brought back down to earth – not by a teammate – but by Alvarez himself.

This time around Alvarez was doing the opposite, pumping up the players and showing them they were able to win many of their games. According to Hein, their head coach spoke at length about their strengths and why they had a chance to compete and break-through in his fourth season at the helm.

"That was a huge contrast from three seasons earlier," Hein said, who played in 10 games during the 1992 season and blocked a punt in UW's 19-16 win against Purdue. "It was almost like he was trying to convince us that we could

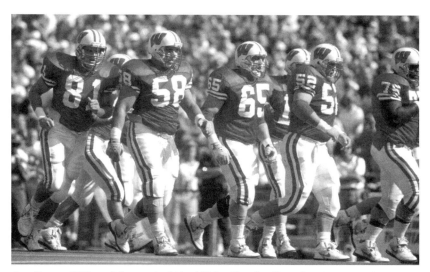

Joe Panos (58) and the rest of the 1993 offensive line. | University of Wisconsin Archives

win. We're not the doormat anymore. We were close last year, but it doesn't necessarily need to be close. We match-up at every position with the teams we're going to be playing, so right away that was a huge confidence builder for all of us because we always viewed Coach Alvarez as a straight shooter. For him to say that, at least to me, meant a lot."

Prior to the season, as with every year, the players selected their captains. The team nominated Shackerford, who recorded 77 tackles, 14 for loss, along with five sacks in 1992. The other nomination went to the former walk-on from Brookfield, Panos. The evolution from a starting Division III defensive tackle to one of the most respected players on a potent Big Ten squad was nearly complete.

"He turned into a leader. From the end of his junior year to his senior year he took over a strong leadership role. He just took it over. In the summer there were incidents where he stepped up, and wasn't going to let some things go," acknowledged Alvarez. "I think the guys really followed him. He was mature, and he backed up everything he said. The guys respected that."

According to Rudolph, the future NFL third-round draft pick was one of the first guys to "really have an edge," and who also gave a voice of leadership to the offensive line. He wasn't afraid to speak up about toughness.

"That type of stuff was huge at the time," Rudolph said. "It kind of set the tone and the direction of that team as things came up and as the season moved forward. I would say that was great value. I think anytime you speak or anytime you open your mouth, people are going to look at what you're doing. He always backed up what he said in a huge way and made it fun."

Wisconsin would start the season with six consecutive wins.

The Sunday after a 24-16 win at SMU, another milestone was reached. UW entered at No. 24 in the AP Top 25 and No. 25 in the USA Today Coaches poll. The Badgers, for the first time since 1984, were ranked. They would continue to rack up the wins and run their undefeated streak to four with a 27-15 road win against the Indiana Hoosiers.

After that road win, a reporter questioned Panos as to whether Wisconsin could really compete to be a player in the Big Ten with Michigan and Ohio State. The captain retorted in one of the now-legendary lines in UW history:

Why not Wisconsin?

"Joe's deal was, 'Okay, I'm going to say what I want, and I can back it up. Now, you're either with me or against me, but you're not going to stand on the sidelines,'" said former Wisconsin assistant Jim Hueber, who coached the running backs from 1992-94 and offensive linemen from 1995-2005. "I think that attitude, more than anything, helped out, but we also had good defensive guys like Mike Thompson and Shack and those guys. They had all been around. The defense knew they were pretty good. I think Joe gave the offense a confidence when he said that."

The Badgers would avenge 1992's loss against the Wildcats, dismantling Northwestern 53-14 in Madison, then knocked off the Boilermakers 42-28 in West Lafayette. Six up, six down, as UW would move up to No. 15 in the AP poll, and No. 12 in the USA Today/CNN Coaches' poll. They would run into a setback in the Twin Cities the following week, however.

Despite out gaining the Gophers 605-385 in total yards and Bevell breaking the single game record for passing yards (a record that still stands), the transfer quarterback would throw five costly interceptions. Along with a fumble, Wisconsin would commit six turnovers total in a 28-21 loss. Missed opportunities would compound the frustrating loss with kicker John Hall missing field goals of 30 and 38 yards.

The Badgers would still have the chance to put themselves in position for Pasadena. Michigan lost in the final minute against Illinois in a 24-21 stunner at the "Big House" in Ann Arbor.

Both teams were down after losing the previous week, but the scene was set for a huge contest in Madison.

UW started the scoring with two field goals in the first and second quarters, but they wouldn't come from the cannon-legged Hall. A redshirt freshman who was named the starter after Thompson departed, Hall started the season 1-for-6, including going 0-for-4 on attempts between 30 and 39 yards. Alvarez and Norvell would turn over placekicking duties for shorter field goals and PATs to walk-on Rick Schnetzky. When No. 98 jogged onto the field, he was a fresh face that no one knew.

"(ESPN play-by-play voice) Brad Nessler was sitting in my office, and he said to me, 'Who's kicking today?' I only gave him the number. He asked, 'Well who is it?' I said, 'I don't know, but he just walked on. You'll know his name after this game because he can kick," Alvarez said with a huge laugh.

Schnetzky's development as a college football player didn't start until November 1991. He never played organized football until he walked on the spring of 1993. During Thanksgiving break after watching a kicker miss some extra points, the soccer player realized he wanted to try his hand at putting the pigskin through the uprights.

Schnetzky made tapes of his kicking escapades and sent them out to 40 college football teams, hearing back from many, but not Wisconsin. So he took matters into his own hands.

He would find out the coaches' schedules in hopes that he could get their attention inside the McClain Center as he kicked field goals. The noise made when the balls hit the side of the building gave off a loud, clanging noise noticeable to all inside the facility.

Eventually, the 5-foot-10, 170-pound specialist got the attention of Wisconsin athletic official – and former Badger and NFL kicker – Jim Bakken. After watching him kick, Bakken notified the coaches and Schnetzky found his way onto the roster that spring.

Schnetzky traveled to SMU and to Minnesota, and would only convert an extra point against Northwestern after Hall missed a couple of conversions. No consistent role would be set for the former hockey aficionado until the big match-up against the Wolverines. The Mequon native found out the Thursday before the game that he would handle the placekicking duties for short field goals in what was arguably the biggest contest of the season. It would take some nudging on his part to get the kicking change made.

"John was just struggling and I was making my kicks," Schnetzky recalled. "Finally, I was walking off after practice on Wednesday, and I pulled Coach Norvell aside and said, 'Coach Norvell, no disrespect, but if you're not going to play me, I don't need to be on this football team.'"

Rich Schnetzky (98) attempts a field goal during practice. | Wisconsin State Journal

"I don't remember that specific conversation," Norvell admitted. "I know this – he was a really competitive kid. I know he wanted to play, and he was always prepared to play. I do remember there was some competition between those guys. It never bothered me that kids spoke up like that because they have got a lot invested and are trying to compete and have confidence in themselves. He lined up for some pretty big kicks and that's because he earned that right."

After seeing his scholarship kicker struggle, Alvarez asked Norvell if the walk-on was ready. He also inquired if the overly-confident Schnetzky was bugging him repeatedly for game time action. According to the head coach, Norvell conceded the kid was. The head coach had heard enough – he'd get his shot.

"I was just worried it would be too big for him, the stage," Alvarez recalled, "but he was cocky as hell. He wanted to kick. As soon as I found out he was bugging Jay that he should be kicking, I said he should be kicking."

"I'll never forget walking off the field. I get goose bumps right now even thinking about it. Vince Zullo walked up to me and goes, 'You're kicking against Michigan,'" Schnetzky reminisced with a laugh. "Next thing I know, Coach Norvell pulled me aside and said, 'You know what, we're going to start you against Michigan. Be ready.'"

So there he was, attempting to put the Badgers on the scoreboard with over six minutes left in the first quarter in the biggest game of the season. His first ever collegiate field goal attempt was a chip-shot, 25-yarder. There would also be a new holder, as Schnetzky was a left-footed kicker. Hall was a righty.

"For me, you're confident that you've done this so many times that you feel comfortable with the snap and hold, and you'll be able to take care of business," Schnetzky said. "You just go out there, it's so overwhelming. There's so much stuff going on, you don't hear anything. You only see where the ball's coming from, and you kind of go into default mode.

"Luckily for me, it was two short kicks and Michigan

didn't know what to expect because now (starting quarterback Darrell) Bevell is the holder, and they have to worry about a fake. There wasn't a lot of pressure with those kicks, and when I look back at it, it was the perfect situation for me to get a couple of kicks under my belt."

Schnetzky would connect on both of his field goal attempts of 25 and 26 yards in the first half to put Wisconsin up 6-0. The staple of the Wisconsin offense was its rushing attack, as it gained 225 yards. Moss would rush for 128, one of his 11 consecutive games of over 100 yards. Fletcher ran for 78 yards on nine carries, including a 12-yard touchdown to put the Badgers up by 10 at halftime.

The Wolverines' offense, led by quarterback Todd Collins, brought the game within a field goal after a seven-yard touchdown pass to Derrick Alexander late in the third quarter. Wisconsin would nurse the three-point lead, as two turnovers forced by the Badgers deep in its own territory kept the lead intact.

Collins pushed his offense down to the UW 21-yard line with over five minutes left in the contest, but it would ultimately be the closest they'd get to threatening to score. On a 4th-and-8 from UW's 28-yard line, Collins completed a pass to wide receiver Walter Smith. Hein and Unverzagt tackled the Wolverine for only a seven-yard gain, forcing a turnover on downs.

Outside linebacker Chris Hein (50) in action. | University of Wisconsin Archives

Wisconsin ran out the final 5:14 on the clock, and would beat the Wolverines 13-10 on that late October afternoon.

On the field, it was one of the greatest memories Hein would have.

"The Michigan game was huge. I was named Player of the Game by WTMJ radio, which was really special for me," acknowledged Hein, whose hometown, Plymouth, was just an hour north of Milwaukee. "I'd grown up listening to 620 WTMJ for Bucks, Brewers and Badger games my whole life. They interviewed me the Monday after the game live on the radio station. That was to me, personally, one of the highlights of my career. With the stop and the quarterback pressure earlier in that drive, I had the opportunity to make some plays in that game."

It was another defining moment for the football program under Alvarez, and an extreme high after a tough loss to Minnesota a week earlier. Players were excited, exchanging post-game pleasantries with fans and family. Some coaches and media were already going towards the locker room and post-game interview sessions. They didn't notice the mad rush from students on to the field from student sections O, P, and Q, a flood of what was reportedly 12,000 fans that would ultimately overwhelm the railing and chain link fences.

The celebrations turned into a tragedy. Students were trapped under each other after trying to get onto the field, being crushed and suffocated due to the piles of people above them. Badgers players saw the potential catastrophe happening and tried to help. Panos, Rudolph, offensive lineman Brian Patterson, and others tried to pull the students from the human wreckage.

Panos and Rudolph were among those helping and credited with saving lives among the 70 or more injured, but another player would receive nationwide attention for his efforts in helping fans in the post-game frenzy. Walk-on wide receiver, Michael Brin, saved a couple of students, even performing mouth-to-mouth resuscitation on a young woman who was blue in the face.

His efforts on the field that day earned him ABC's

"Newsmaker of the Week." Reporters from the *Chicago Tribune, Los Angeles Times* and the *New York Times* all listened in to the conversation Brin had with one of the people he assisted in Aimee Jansen. It's a series of stories the current co-offensive coordinator of the Kansas City Chiefs still recalls to this day when asked about that Saturday.

"Just the fact he was able to help somebody, maybe save their life that day on one of the greatest days of football – beating the University of Michigan – and then have that go on afterwards – it was neat to have him be a part of that," Brad Childress said. "I haven't communicated with him (since Brin left Wisconsin football), but always felt very proud about what he did that day."

No one perished in the midst of the chaos that ensued inside the stadium that day, and Wisconsin would continue to move along their path to Pasadena with a date with the Ohio State Buckeyes.

UW drove the ball 65 yards in its final drive and would have the chance to kick a field goal for the win, but Schnetzky's 33-yard attempt was blocked by Marlon Kerner, forcing a 14-14 tie. No longer controlling their own destiny, UW would need the Buckeyes to stumble along the way to regain the inside track to the Rose Bowl.

Luckily, their final two games were spread out over four weeks, as Wisconsin had two more bye weeks on their schedule. Even more fortunate, the Badgers would receive help from the Wolverines as they would take care of the Buckeyes in a 28-0 win on November 20. If UW won out, Pasadena would be in their sights.

The Badgers blew out the Illini 35-10 in Champaign, with Panos and company opening up holes for Moss and Fletcher to the tune of 301 yards on the ground against the No. 4 rushing defense in the nation.

After another week of rest, the Badgers would head to Tokyo for their final regular season conference game. According to Alvarez in his autobiography *Don't Flinch,* team personnel spoke with professors from the university who were consultants for NASA on how to prepare for the 6,000-mile trip and 15 hour time difference.

"That game in Japan was an amazing experience, and the preparation for that game is legendary," Hein remembered. "You want to talk about Coach Alvarez's attention to detail. It was just insane. The level we went through for the trip alone, from talking to NASA and conversations about how they prepare the astronauts. They were charting when we had to wear sunglasses leading up to the trip, at what hour and for how long each day, to kind of train our brains for the time change when we arrived in Tokyo. We were on Tokyo time in Madison three days before we left."

That included not sleeping on the flight until they arrived in Tokyo.

"They won that game at 55,000 feet on the way to Tokyo," Manthey stated. "The coaches had that team prepared."

Michigan State held a 7-3 lead into the second quarter, but the Badgers reeled off 21 straight points to take a commanding 24-7 lead and never looked back. The offense racked up 521 yards and four rushing touchdowns. Both Fletcher and Moss went over 100 yards again. Schnetzky converted field goals from 27 and 34 yards, and Veit didn't even have to attempt a punt.

Celebrations would ensue as the Badgers walloped the Spartans 41-20.

The *Wisconsin State Journal's* front page on Sunday, December 5 declared "BIG RED ROSES!" in commemoration of the team's achievement.

Wisconsin fans would welcome back the returning Badgers at Camp Randall Stadium, but many found ways to surprise and congratulate their team even before they got back to the state capital.

"We're driving back from Chicago on I-90," Manthey explained, "and as we get into Wisconsin at the bottom of each of the entrance ramps, cars were parked and people were sitting there waving and cheering and holding signs up because they knew the Badgers' buses would be driving past those exit ramps. That one really took me back a bit as to how much it meant to people."

Schnetzky was also taken aback by the fans on the freeway near the Wisconsin-Illinois border.

"It hits you like a ton of bricks," he recalled. "All the people in Wisconsin care about is finally having a winning football team. They've driven, walked, crawled to the middle of nowhere to have one second to wave to the bus, because that's what kind of people are in Wisconsin and what type of fans Wisconsin Badger fans are. It was amazing."

****

After returning from Japan, the Badgers got back to work preparing for the Rose Bowl. UCLA was ranked 14th in the nation, and there wasn't a lot of respect being given to Wisconsin, who just finished the regular season 9-1-1.

Bruins head coach Terry Donahue even asked Alvarez if his team could dress in their own locker room as the Rose Bowl was where UCLA played its home games during the year. As Wisconsin was technically the home squad and the UW head coach was always looking for an edge on his opponent, he swiftly denied Donahue's request.

"We obviously felt we were disrespected going out there by pretty much the entire West Coast," Hein said. "I remember some fans coming up to us saying, 'You guys are just a bunch of farmers from Wisconsin. You're going to get it handed to you by UCLA,' and stuff like that. So that helped motivate us to remember why we were there, and winning the game was the most important thing and to not get caught up in the other stuff, the banquets, the (Lawry's) Beef Bowl, the city and all that."

UW would be focused headed into their match-up against the Bruins, and the Badger faithful would be there to support them. Alvarez remembers his limo driver for the week in Los Angeles, a former UCLA student body president, telling him Wisconsin fans were scooping up as many tickets as were available.

"I told the kids this was going to be like Camp Randall

West," Alvarez said.

"Our people were buying anything that moved. When you walk out on that field you're going to feel like you're in Camp Randall because the stadium is going to be yours. We're in home red. We got the majority of the people. It was pretty cool."

Wisconsin received the opening kickoff and would start their first drive from their own 20-yard line. Though the drive didn't end with points on the board, they moved it to the UCLA 41 before punting. Veit would hit it at the 10-yard line, and with some friendly bounces, the ball was downed at the two by Vince Zullo.

It would be a proud moment for the Veit family, as Sam's father, Gene Veit, had punted in the 1957 Rose Bowl game for Iowa. For the Racine native, pinning opponents deep in their own territory was a strength. Out of 39 punts in the 1993 season, six would be downed inside the 20-yard line, one inside the 10, and an impressive seven would be downed inside the 5-yard line.

Many of his punts that year were downed by fellow walk-ons Zullo, Wirth and Chad Cascadden. Great special teams play was a calling card of some of the early Alvarez squads.

"They are seemingly little things that don't show up on the highlight reel very much but it was a real big deal for Barry's teams," Wisconsin radio voice Matt Lepay said. "He always talked about the hidden yards, the field position battle, and guys like Manley, Zullo, Cascadden and Wirth had big roles. They helped tilt the field in the Badgers' favor on a number of occasions."

Zullo was all of 5-foot-10, 185 pounds, an all-conference selection from Westosha High School. A back-up wide receiver, he was regarded as one of the best special teams players in his time at Wisconsin and earned the Special Teams Player of the Year award in 1992. The Salem, Wis., product contributed 24 career tackles on special teams between 1991-94.

Cascadden was a standout on special teams but he saw substantial playing time on defense as well. The Chippewa

Falls native initially walked on to Wisconsin as a defensive back but was moved to linebacker his junior year. He and Hein would work interchangeably in that "drop" linebacker spot during their final two years at UW. In 1993, he registered 17 tackles, three for loss, in 12 games.

Wirth contributed on special teams from 1990-93 and finished his playing career with 34 tackles. He started his college career in Morton's last season at Wisconsin, and slowly built his way up to contributing on many of the special teams units each Saturday as well as serving as the backup fullback to Montgomery. The four-year letterman was given the nickname "The White Rat" from Aaron Norvell, Jay's brother and a former UW linebacker. Wirth himself doesn't know why he was bestowed such a distinction, though many former teammates laugh when recalling the name and its variations.

"If you didn't have a nickname, you were in trouble so everybody had a nickname," Jay Norvell explained. "It was just so easy to call him the 'White Rat' because he was so pale and albino and white hair and everything. It was the perfect nickname for him. If you were around at all, you would get a nickname pretty quick."

Wirth would be needed in the offensive backfield against the Bruins for the last quarter-and-a-half of the Rose Bowl. With just over eight minutes left in the third quarter, Moss was halted for a one-yard loss on a 4th-and-1 run. A fight broke out after the tackle between Wisconsin wide receiver Lee DeRamus and Montgomery, and UCLA safety Donovan Gallitin and Goodwin. There should have been a flag on the play, as Donnie Edwards of the Bruins was offsides, but the refs didn't throw it.

All four players would be ejected for the rest of the game. Wirth's worth would be shown yet again as one of UW's unsung heroes.

"There wasn't any apprehension at all because we did have some two fullback sets, and we were a power, 'grind it out kind of football team as well," Wirth said, when asked about stepping up. "Coach Alvarez always talked about things happening during the game and you having to be ready to go, ready to adjust to adversity. That happens in every football game throughout the season. When you're out there, you're called upon to step up and get after it."

"When Wirth came in, nobody flinched," Rudolph said. "Everybody had great faith that he would do a great job. You're talking about losing Montgomery, an NFL drafted guy, an outstanding player and Mark was a huge part in how we performed that year. When the "White Rat" came in, we said, 'Okay, let's go.' I don't know how many teams would feel the same. That's the type of confidence we had in him because of the way he worked. We trusted him."

The Badgers' defense would bend but not break that afternoon. They gave up 500 yards to the Bruins, including 14 catches for 176 yards to Stokes. Though UCLA marched up and down the field, UW forced six turnovers that translated to 14 points. They'd get the ball back late in the game, down 21-16 and starting at their own 38. Cook moved the Bruins down to the 18-yard line in seven plays. UW's defense needed just one more stop to notch the program's first Rose Bowl win, but it was a daunting task.

"The last drive, I was just gassed out there because they were throwing the ball every down, and I was just rushing the passer at that time," Hein said. "I think we were in nickel on defense, I was pretty

Jeff Wirth | University of Wisconsin Athletics

much just trying to hold on."

Cook finished the game, completing 28-of-43 passes for 288 yards, but made a critical error on what would be the final play of the game. Rather than throwing the ball away, the Bruins signal caller ran the ball for a three-yard gain. Mike Thompson made the tackle, but sat on him to allow more time to run off the clock. Before they could get the ball centered and snapped, time expired.

On the television broadcast, replays showed the camera focused in on Alvarez staring at that game clock. When the scoreboard hit zero, his arms went up in triumph as Wisconsin defeated UCLA 21-16. Bedlam ensued as Manthey proudly announced, "The greatest win in Badgers' history, and the greatest game in Wisconsin history is no longer a loss!" a reference to UW's legendary 42-37 loss to the USC Trojans in the 1963 Rose Bowl.

Four years earlier, winning the Rose Bowl was unimaginable. On New Year's Day 1994, the Badgers were co-Big Ten, and more importantly, Rose Bowl champions.

Celebrations ensued for the tens of thousands of Wisconsin fans who flocked to Pasadena to witness history. The 1993 team took Wisconsin to new heights in college football, but it was the years of rebuilding, laying the foundation into the program that really solidified Badgers football for generations to come. For walk-ons like Panos, Hein, Cascadden, Veit, Schnetzky, Zullo and Wirth, their contributions that season and in Alvarez' early years set the standard for what walk-ons in the UW program could accomplish.

"Those were great, great times," Norvell recalled, who's now the offensive passing game coordinator and wide receivers coach at Arizona State. "A lot of those kids earned scholarships and were really the backbone – the life blood – of the turnaround at Wisconsin. When you think about going from 1-10 to 10-1-1 and going to the Rose Bowl, all of those guys were a huge part of that. They were guys that started as walk-ons but they were part of the fiber, the backbone and the grit of that turnaround at Wisconsin. They didn't have the name value of a Darrell Bevell or Brent Moss or Terrell Fletcher, but those guys were every bit as important in turning that program around because they were really the heartbeat of the team by how hard they played."

Badger players celebrate following the 1994 Rose Bowl. | AP Photo

CHAPTER THREE

Rebuilding the Road to Pasadena

After that euphoric 1993 season, Wisconsin went on to boast winning records in three of its next four seasons and two more bowl wins. An expectation of winning became the norm for the Alvarez regime, along with competing for conference championships and trips to Pasadena. The team, however, wouldn't win more than eight games from 1995-97.

The 1997 campaign was a struggle towards the end, but would later fuel a great resurgence and pinnacle of success that has not been duplicated by any Big Ten program. The Badgers battled through to an 8-5 record, 5-3 in conference play. After starting the year with eight wins in their first ten games, UW dropped three straight to end their season. Those losses included a 26-16 loss to No. 1 and Associated Press national champion Michigan, a 35-10 loss at top ten ranked Penn State, and to Georgia on New Year's Day. The embarrassing loss to the Bulldogs left a bitter taste in the players' mouths. Though earning a spot in a New Year's Day bowl, the team wasn't satisfied with their performances. Just four years earlier, Wisconsin captured its first ever Rose Bowl title against UCLA.

There would be some key pieces coming back for the 1998 campaign, and with some young talent gaining experience, the team goal became evident. In early 1998, left tackle

Chris McIntosh declared he didn't come to Wisconsin to go to the Outback Bowl, but came to win the Big Ten Championship and play in the Rose Bowl.

"The goal that was set made it clear that being mediocre and just making a bowl game was not what everybody wanted, and I thought that was powerful because everybody bought in," former right tackle Mark Tauscher pointed out, then a reserve offensive lineman. "It was almost like a light went on. We don't have to be average, we can set this goal higher with the defense that we had, and with Ron Dayne and the running game that we figured we would have. Why not?"

Years earlier, "Why not Wisconsin?" rang throughout the halls of campus from Panos' glorified quote. Now, a new generation of Badgers would begin to sprint, lift, and train on a different level than before.

Under strength and conditioning coach John Dettmann, activities and training regiments were turned up a notch to mold and shape the players. Walk-ons like Donnel Thompson, Bobby Adamov and Jason Doering emerged as leaders throughout these sessions.

The extra work put in by this special group of student-athletes led to a remarkable two years for the Wisconsin football program. With at least four consistent starters and two captains on each team during the 1998 and 1999 seasons being former walk-ons, the blue-collared and physical nature of these Badgers teams formed an identity that guided them to back-to-back Rose Bowl championships.

Thompson remembered a new routine that according to Dettmann, would develop "power, stride length and intestinal fortitude." The football team's strength and conditioning coach employed a new tactic to make the muscles twitch and burn a little sharper. The players began to run the steps in the upper decks of Camp Randall.

There was quite a difference between the two tiers of stadium steps. The lower deck had shorter lengths between steps, while Thompson noted the series of upper deck steps doubled or tripled in height, essentially becoming a running lunge. Dettman saw the value in developing power with each player through this exercise, forcing players to lift their legs higher and exert more energy. He referred to these "stadiums" as a rite of passage that would bring old and young teammates alike together, whether completing the daunting task on their own or dragging someone up and down the stairs to do so.

"If you were going to play football at Wisconsin," Dettman stated, "this was something you were going to have to do and accomplish to be considered one of the players."

It was part of the initiative to become leaner and quicker in hopes of matching up with more athletic teams. Friday morning workouts included agility drills, pushing sleds and grinding out bear crawls on the incline ramp, which led up to a sign bearing the phrase, "The Road to the Rose Bowl Begins Here." It was the same tunnel the players would walk out of on game day.

"It was just kind of a refocus," Tauscher admitted. "I think it was more of we had gotten stagnant. Let's freshen it up and let's test ourselves not just physically, but mentally. And there were some workouts that were real hard. The summer was just great, and it brought everybody together."

That wouldn't be enough, however. Dettman recalls a disappointing conditioning sessions with the team. He made his displeasure known that day after the team ran the upper decks. Rather than sulk, a group of players took it upon themselves, realizing they weren't where they needed to be to compete among the elite of the conference.

There was a knock on the door of Dettmann's residence at 6:30 the next morning. He opened his front door to see fullback Cecil Martin, Thompson and a band of 30-plus Badgers, in trucks and vehicles, wanting to train.

Dettmann's response was swift: "I'll be with you in 10 seconds. Let me get a pair of shorts on, and let's go."

In a neighborhood near current-day Fitchburg, players would sprint up a 300-foot incline on a street that ascended to a peak. Dettman would start the team with four sprints up, then progress in increments up to eight sprints. Former men's basketball coach Bo Ryan would make his teams annually face Elver Park's famed hill to build endurance for a 30-plus game schedule, but this hill located off of Adobe Way in southwestern Madison, was *the* hill.

Ryan's conditioning was a part of the basketball team's annual tradition, but for this select group of football players, it wasn't *mandatory*. This was asked for *by the players*. A look at the current day street shows a slice of near suburban tranquility, with homes and lawns fit for middle-class Wisconsinites. Though charming, it's an ingrained landmark that still floods Thompson's memories of hot days and hellacious training.

"There's no way you can forget that hill," Thompson acknowledged.

"I remember it like it was yesterday," Dettmann reminisced glowingly, admitting goose bumps flare up when he thinks back to that day. "We got done and I called everyone up that was there, and there were probably 30-plus guys and I said, 'You guys will win a game this year that you do not deserve to win because you did this.'"

****

Wisconsin's offense rolled over opponents by putting up 31.8 points and 215 yards rushing per contest, while the defense built a wall around each end zone they defended. The Badgers held opponents scoring to just 11.9 points per game, amongst the best in the nation. Seven of Wisconsin's 12 opponents failed to score seven or more points against defensive coordinator Kevin Cosgrove's unit, which also had two shutouts.

Offenses could not score through the air against the pass defense of the Badgers, who allowed only eight passing touchdowns the entire season. They intercepted opposing quarterbacks 19 times. Jamar Fletcher emerged as a playmaking cornerback in picking off seven passes, three of which he returned for touchdowns.

Of the top five tacklers on that 1998 squad, three initially came to UW without athletic scholarships. Thompson, the tough-nosed inside linebacker, led the team with 109. Five out of the 12 games that season Thompson recorded double-digit stops, including 17 against Michigan.

He didn't travel far to play collegiately, but came with a large chip on his shoulder. A Madison native, he played his prep ball at Madison West High School under his father, Curtis. His mother Barbara was the principal. Both Donnel and his brother, Bryson, played for their dad heading into the elder son's junior year. Letters and calls came in from Big Ten schools wanting to keep tabs on him. Invites for each respective school's summer camps would be sent to them.

It was an exciting time for the all-area and all-conference athlete, but an injury would derail Thompson's final prep season. Early in his senior year Thompson broke his right arm. The break was devastating – the bone was two to three inches apart. Surgery was needed, and a plate was inserted.

"Literally, the next day, calls stopped. Letters stopped, and I didn't hear from any of the schools anymore," Thompson said. "I think a couple of Division III schools were still interested, a couple of Division II schools like Northern Michigan were still interested. It was a pretty depressing time in my life."

The buzz from other schools was gone, but Wisconsin maintained interest. Assistant coach John Palermo made the mile-long trek to West to speak with the future Badger. Inside the gym, the defensive line coach offered Thompson a preferred walk-on position, noting he'd get every opportunity to showcase his skills on the field. He would take the opportunity given to him and return to the stadium he used to sell sodas at in his earlier years.

Though grateful for the chance to compete to play on Saturdays in front of tens of thousands of fans, Thompson's desire to get on the field quickly at the next level was apparent. He would arrive early before practice to warm up and go through mental and physical drills, often confirming his assignments and his footwork. At night, the freshman would do his own version of homework, creating flashcards with each defense on one side. On the other side would be Thompson's responsibilities, both against the run and the pass. The teaching tool helped immensely, as it minimized mental errors on the field and allowed the under-recruited linebacker to work his way up the depth chart. He would travel with the team as primarily a special team's contributor in his first season as a Badger, playing in all 13 games.

It didn't remove that chip on his shoulder, however.

"Yeah, I was pissed," Thompson admitted when asked about his motivational drive. "There's no doubt about it. I felt like there were players that my talent was equal with – and they were on scholarship and I wasn't.

"I took it personally. Every day, I was determined to prove to the University of Wisconsin and every other school that passed on me that they made a mistake at the time. I was very, very fortunate that Wisconsin opened the doors and let me come walk-on, but I wanted to show that I deserved a scholarship."

His reward for his early contributions was the one that fueled his drive early on. Cosgrove called Thompson into his office. Thompson himself described the ordeal as odd at first, thinking "the only time being called up into his office was to yell at me." This time would be different.

Donnel Thompson (44) sacks the Penn State quarterback. | Wisconsin State Journal

He placed a phone call to Donnel's father, who taught him the ins and outs of the game, announcing the good news. He wouldn't have to worry about paying for college because Donnel was getting put on scholarship. It was a special moment shared between father and a son.

That 1997 season Thompson further asserted himself as a staple of the Badgers' defense, becoming a regular starter in Cosgrove's 4-3 scheme. Asserting himself may be an understatement, as Thompson led the team in tackles with 141 stops, an individual performance that ranks 13th on Wisconsin's single-season record list. It may have been a revelation to those watching the program from the outside, but his teammates knew that every play was a battle Thompson wanted to win.

"I can pretty much say any 9-on-7 (drill), I probably got a headache from Donnel," former scholarship guard Bill Ferrario said. "Being a guard, power was my play that I pulled on. I pulled from the back side to the front side, and led up the hole. I was always taking on a linebacker, and 50 percent of the time, it was Donnel."

Respect for Adamov and Thompson grew amongst their teammates and peers going into the 1998 season. The two combined for 218 tackles in 1997. When captains were nominated, fullback Cecil Martin and McIntosh were honored with that distinction, along with the two linebackers and friends – whose work ethic, mentality and physical style of play epitomized Wisconsin football. Until that season, left tackle Joe Panos was the only walk-on who was voted to be a captain by his peers during the Alvarez era. Now, half of the Badgers' captains were walk-ons.

"Those guys were great leaders," Alvarez said. "Everybody admired them. Donnel came in as a tough guy right away and a student of the game. Bobby just grew into someone people respected. We had a lot of guys that worked hard. They were examples of it."

"That affirmation of being named a captain holds a special place because it's recognized and it's voted on by peers," Adamov admitted. "Even going through my life just personally and professionally, I still look back on that honor as one of the greatest I've been afforded."

****

Adamov recorded 83 stops during his senior season, placing him fifth on the team. That included a season-high 23 against Purdue on October 10, which was the first game when House of Pain's "Jump Around" played throughout Camp Randall Stadium – a tradition that continues to this day. Adamov was a four-year letter winner at Wisconsin from 1995-98, arriving in Madison a season after UW's Rose Bowl championship. He came from Southern Door High School, a half-hour northeast of Green Bay that would produce NFL-capable players in Jim Flanigan, Al and Ben Johnson.

Despite boasting all-state defensive back honors as a senior, no Big Ten offers came. He flew out west to Fargo to visit then-Division II North Dakota State, and was offered. However, he traveled to Madison in hopes the Badgers' coaching staff would do the same. Unfortunately, he

wouldn't come home with an offer in hand. Adamov was told the coaching staff was looking to offer a player who could play safety and cornerback, something they felt his game wouldn't translate to at the Division I level.

"I remember feeling a little bit deflated as I was leaving there

Bob Adamov (29) closes in for the tackle. | Wisconsin State Journal because I wanted to go to Wisconsin," Adamov admitted, who earned 10 letters between three prep sports. "On the way home, I made the decision that I was going to go to North Dakota State. There was scholarship money on the table that would pay for my schooling, and that was what I was going to do."

Word got back to McCarney that the all-state player would be heading out to Fargo to play for the Bison. He called the high school and got in touch with Adamov, wanting to sit down and talk with him before the all-conference player made his final decision. Making the three-hour trek northeast to sell Wisconsin, McCarney persuaded Adamov to walk-on.

He redshirted his freshman year in 1994 but worked his way into the two-deep heading into the 1995 spring game. He continued his momentum towards significant playing time in the spring game as the strong safety intercepted a Bevell pass and rumbled for the touchdown. The Door County native admitted that play of the game was a defining point of his collegiate football career.

Adamov made some emergency starts that year where he tallied 18 tackles in place of an injured Leonard Taylor, then became a regular starter at strong safety in 1996. He racked up 77 tackles and would be one of Wisconsin's top five tacklers for the next three years.

That streak continued, even with a position change that forced him to move closer to the line of scrimmage. Adamov had played defensive back his first three seasons at Wisconsin, but new secondary coach Phil Elmassian had other plans. A former defensive coordinator under Frank Beamer at Virginia Tech from 1993-94, "Coach Elmo" took over instructing the cornerbacks and safeties.

Adamov sat down with Elmassian in his office to talk about some new defensive schemes. Rather than discussing new alignments and plays, Elmassian explained that his typical safeties were lighter than the 220-pound Adamov by about 40 pounds. Adamov wondered what that meant for him, as he had played defensive back since high school.

"He's like, 'That means you're an outside linebacker now, so go next door.' So I actually got fired from strong safety and I had to go next door." Adamov said with a laugh. "I went over there [to the outside linebackers]. It was great. I got to work under and be with Coach Jay Hayes, and he was fantastic."

"Well he just kept getting a little bit bigger," Hayes, then the outside linebackers coach from 1995-98, confirmed. "He played hard, and just did things the right way, and was always there and took care of his business. Nothing flashy, but had really good ball skills."

Adamov flourished in his new role, having the flexibility to play man coverage and blanket opposing offenses. The Southern Door product continued his presence as one of Wisconsin's more respected leaders. The player who was not offered a single Division I scholarship and who was set to become a Bison at a Division II program just a few years earlier was thriving as a Big Ten linebacker.

"As I look back in life," Adamov said, "I'm glad that I didn't go to North Dakota State because I think UW has done so much for me as an individual."

****

Jason Doering, a native of Rhinelander, was a regular starter at free safety from 1998-2000. The two-time captain's presence enhanced a potent secondary. He tied for second on the team with three interceptions, and his 94 tackles placed him fourth on the team behind Thompson.

Doering almost didn't come to Madison, or play football for that matter. There were limited recruiting opportunities for him on the gridiron in his prep days, partly due to the geographical location of Rhinelander in extreme northern Wisconsin. Admittedly, he was also a late bloomer. Division II schools like Northern Michigan and Michigan Tech called, along with Division III schools within the WIAC. Another sport set him on a path across the Wisconsin-Illinois border, however.

Doering was a standout not just on the football field but under the lights of the baseball diamond. His baseball coach had connections from his days in the Los Angeles Dodgers' minor league organization. The future NFL veteran was ready to try to make his mark on

Jason Doering (8) delivers another hard hitting tackle. | Wisconsin State Journal

the diamond at Triton College just outside of Chicago.

"A lot of the opportunities are like most anything in life, it's being at the right place at the right time," Doering acknowledged. "When you have an opportunity and take advantage of it, that helps get you noticed."

His opportunity came during the annual Shrine Bowl game in 1996. The all-star game featured some of the state's best high school players. According to Doering, future teammates like Chris Ghidorzi and Ross Kolodziej mentioned his name to the UW coaching staff, and soon after, assistants began reaching out to him. Doering negotiated his way onto starting with the team during camp, rather than coming in during the semester. He redshirted his first year and allowed Dettmann's training routines to mold him into a stronger, faster, and more agile player. The former strength and conditioning coach recalled the dedication, intensity, and vigor Doering displayed not just his first year, but throughout his career.

"You talk about a guy who was a warrior," Dettmann said. "It didn't matter what kind of work was going to go down that day. He wasn't going to turn it down. In other words, he was going to attack everything. Those kinds of guys have tremendous success because they know nothing's given to you, you have to earn it all."

Frustrations set in for the young defensive back, however, going into his redshirt freshman season. The infusion of Elmassian as secondary coach breathed new life into the position group. The door was open for anyone who could play during spring ball. Doering capitalized on the opportunity and worked himself into the two-deep on the Badgers' depth chart. Incumbent Bobby Myers was still the starting free safety.

During that 1997 season, frustration began to build within Doering. Privately, he made up his mind he would look into baseball, until opportunity struck again on the gridiron. Like many walk-ons, he was just waiting in the wings for a shot to prove himself.

The Michigan Wolverines, ranked No. 1 in the AP poll at the time, strolled into Camp Randall Stadium. With the defense floundering, the coaching staff inserted Doering for Myers during the game without much notice.

"Myers ended up being a really good player for us, but he got beat on a play and had a habit of dropping his head and arms," Alvarez recalled. "I didn't even ask the secondary coach. I said 'Doering, you're in there.'"

"As you watch the replay of that game, Brent Musburger says, 'A star is born tonight,' because he whacked them. He was coming down from that safety spot and making some collisions. Man, he whacked the hell out of people."

"When I look back on it, getting thrown in there was probably the best way to do it because I didn't have time to over think it," Doering said. "Basically, you go into the game, and go play. At this point, they didn't want to watch the other guy play anymore. It's 'you're going in the game – play.'"

It was the beginning of a successful reign in the secondary for the punishing defender. Though the Wolverines defeated the Badgers 26-16 in Madison that Saturday afternoon, Doering asserted himself. In only 44 plays, the redshirt freshman recorded 13 tackles. He followed that performance up with a team-leading nine stops against Penn State the week after, then recorded 13 in the 33-6 loss to Georgia in the Outback Bowl.

It was a huge change in fortune in the final three games of that season for the safety teammates nicknamed "Thumper." He tallied 35 of his 36 tackles against the No. 1, No. 6 and No. 11 teams in the nation, respectively.

"In '97 Michigan won the national title, so it wasn't as if we were playing some school that didn't have many talented guys," Doering said. "This is the best school in the country, so when I was able to play in that game and have the success I had, and then got to start the next three games after that -- I knew at that point that I can play at that level. I can play very well at that level, and I'm good enough to be here."

****

According to Adamov, the players started calling out "Rose Bowl" at the end of the practices during fall camp. Expectations were high, but after about two sessions, Alvarez stopped them. The players needed to focus on one game at a time.

UW would go on to a 10-1 regular season record, 7-1 in conference play. The team won its first three non-conference games, outscoring their opponents 123-21. They would continue their dominance in a 38-7 walloping of Northwestern to start off the conference slate on a positive note. UW would score three touchdowns of over 45 yards each and two scores off of special teams.

Wisconsin overcame a flat start with a gutsy 24-20 comeback win at Indiana on October 3. They battled back to take the lead on a four-yard Dayne touchdown early in the fourth quarter. Doering intercepted an Antwaan Randle El pass with just over a minute left in the game to seal the victory against the Hoosiers.

They also withstood Purdue and quarterback Drew Brees's offensive onslaught a week later. The future NFL superstar completed 55 passes on 83 attempts for 494 yards, but he also threw four interceptions. That included one of Fletcher's three pick-sixes on the year in the third quarter, taking a Brees pass 52 yards to the end zone to break a 17-17 tie. Wisconsin went on to win 31-24. Adamov's 23 tackles led the way on defense.

Dettmann believes that Indiana victory was due to that extra effort they exerted on the hill during conditioning. It also helped them greatly against the Boilermakers and defending 103 offensive plays that evening.

UW would take care of Illinois, Iowa and Minnesota before stumbling in their lone loss of the season, a 27-10 stinker to Michigan in Ann Arbor. Michigan's defense contained Dayne, who was held to only 53 yards on 16 carries. Offensively, the Wolverines dominated the Badgers 476-190 in total yards.

UW wouldn't have Ghidorzi for most of the game with a bad hamstring, and back-up Roger Knight broke his arm early in the game as well. Adamov remembers not being able to stop running back Anthony Thomas and the Michigan offense which had 258 yards on the ground. Adamov hyper-extended his knee during the contest, and the medical staff on the sideline advised him not to go back on the field as they feared a worse injury. That wouldn't fly for the Brussels native.

"I told them politely to give me my damn knee pad back, or I was going to go in without it. They gave it back," Adamov declared. "When I got to the huddle, Doering asked me what was going on, and I said I messed up my knee in the last series and that the training staff didn't think I should go back in. I said, 'Let's enjoy it because it might be something serious, and this could be it for me.' As I'm telling Jason this,

I can see his eyes start to fill up with tears. I think he sensed my concern. As a team, we were really close that year. We really did care about each other."

The Badgers would need to win their last game, plus have Michigan lose in their final regular season match-up against Ohio State to smell roses for the first time in four years. Over halfway through the first quarter, the Buckeyes' 31-16 victory was announced to the 78,964 in attendance.

With the added emotional electricity in the air and a trip back to Pasadena hanging in the balance, all the Badgers had to do was take care of business against the Nittany Lions. With Doering leading the way with 13 tackles and Thompson with 12, they clinched a share of the conference title in a 24-3 win over Penn State. Conference tiebreaker rules allowed Wisconsin, who had last earned a Rose Bowl berth in that 1993 season, to head out west.

****

The Badgers opponent in the Rose Bowl would be a highly talented UCLA team that featured All-American quarterback Cade McNown, who passed for almost 3,500 yards and 25 touchdowns. UCLA was one quarter away from a potential Bowl Championship Series (BCS) national title game bid, but blew a 17-point lead in a 49-45 loss to the Miami Hurricanes. As good as UCLA's offense was, their defense was atrocious, surrendering over 430 yards per game – 689 to Miami alone. Their consolation was facing the Wisconsin Badgers.

Many thought Alvarez's team didn't stand a chance against the Bruins, scoffing at the notion of Wisconsin playing in the Rose Bowl. Broadcaster Craig James did not have kind words for the Badgers, who qualified for the trip to Pasadena via that tiebreaker. Working for CBS at the time, James announced Wisconsin was the worst team to ever play in the Rose Bowl. Talk about your bulletin board material. And just like five seasons earlier, the Badgers faced bias from those who call the City of Angels home.

As Alvarez noted in *Don't Flinch*, there was disrespect coming from all angles. On a tour of Universal Studios, Fletcher was angry when a tour guide couldn't name who UCLA was facing. At a black-tie event that both teams attended, Shatner again popped up as he was the Grand Marshall of the Tournament of Roses parade that year. He spoke all about the Bruins during the event. The head coach was none too pleased.

"So the next day we're waiting to walk on stage and he hands me a signed picture," Alvarez recalled. "I tore it up and threw it at his feet. My wife said, 'You can't just do that.'"

"I said, 'I just did.'"

Prior to the game, players were able to enjoy the Lawry's Beef Bowl, where the two Rose Bowl teams compete to see who can consume the most pounds of delicious prime rib. Players devoured plates and plates full of high-end dining, but also had the ability to explore around town. For some, that included crashing a VIP Hollywood party all due to a case of mistaken identity.

Josh Hunt and Matt Unertl, both reserves at the time, strolled down Sunset Boulevard with a group of fellow players one evening. They walked past the now-closed Miyagi's but wanted to check out Dublin's Irish Pub. According to accounts from the two players, a group that included Chris Wagner, Mark Anelli and Erik Bickerstaff decided to take their chances with the four-to-five security guards at the door. Their curiosity peaked inside a very active club that had some A-list celebrities enjoying themselves.

"Erik Bickerstaff walks up and one of the security guys thought that he was Mike Tyson," Unertl recalled. "[The security guard's] like, 'Mike. Mike Tyson.' He must have known him for some reason. This guy, Erik Bickerstaff, kind of looked like him, but we didn't think he could pass for Tyson. But the security guard is like, 'Yeah you guys, these your buddies? You guys can come in here.'"

These new "Hollywood" Badgers appeared to have

stumbled upon a VIP party for the cast and crew of the movie *Any Given Sunday*.

"So we walk in there, and we go upstairs and there is Cameron Diaz, Jamie Foxx, hip-hop artist Big Pun was in there," Unertl recalled. "[NBA shooting guard] Ron Harper, who at the time was playing for the Lakers, was in there. We were kind of just walking around, but pretty much everyone from the cast and crew was there."

The players were star-struck but tried to stay low key as to not have their true identities revealed. Their brush with the talented stars of the silver screen lasted about 20 minutes according to Unertl, but as he said it was "a once-in-a-lifetime chance."

****

Tens of thousands of Wisconsin fans once again flocked to Pasadena. Doering had 16 tickets for his family and girlfriend. He sat near Adamov, whom he had bonded with during fall camp playing late night games of cribbage. The redshirt sophomore counted his tickets, making sure he had the correct allotment to hand out to those who made the 2,000 mile-plus trek.

And then something popped into his head.

"I was thinking, 'I took care of this person, that person, and this person – and then I look at Bobby and I go, 'You know what? I don't think I got my girlfriend a ticket,'" laughed Doering.

"He kind of looked at me and said, 'Well, there's nothing you can do about it now. It's just time to go play.' I said, 'You're right. She'll figure it out.' I laugh because I'm lucky that my wife is very resourceful, and I have good friends that got her in the game."

Ghidorzi's family supplied Doering's significant other with the extra ticket. Crisis averted for the hard-nosed safety, at least off the field.

The Badgers knew the game would be a shootout, despite having a defense that ranked third in the nation in rushing defense and fifth in total defense heading into the bowl match-up. The high octane Bruins' offense averaged 39.7 points per game. Wide receiver Danny Farmer was himself a former walk-on and volleyball player who worked his way up to All-Pac-10 honors that season. He caught 58 receptions, averaging a whopping 22 yards per catch with nine touchdowns.

Despite UCLA's offensive explosiveness, the Badgers knew their rushing game could exploit the Bruins. As Adamov poignantly stated, it would end up "being a big boy football game, where you just went out whacking people in the mouth."

On the field, McNown got his yardage through the air, accounting for 418 yards and three touchdown passes. Farmer caught seven of McNown's 21 completions for 142 yards. The conference champs traded three touchdowns apiece in the first half. Walk-on placekicker Matt Davenport, a consensus first-team All-Big Ten honoree, converted a 40-yard field goal to put Wisconsin up 24-21 heading into halftime.

"We knew that they were going to get some of their big plays, but we were going to minimize them," Adamov said. "We needed to create some turnovers, because as often as we could get the ball in our offensive guy's hands, they were going to respond and have a great day."

The Bruins committed two turnovers in their final four drives against the Hurricanes, dooming their chances at a national championship berth. Two more would stifle their odds at a Rose Bowl victory against a UW defense that led the nation in turnover margin. The most egregious infraction may have been Fletcher's third pick-six of the year, taking a McNown pass 47 yards to increase Wisconsin's lead to 38-28 in the fourth quarter.

UW's offensive line opened holes all day for Dayne and the running game. The bruising yet nimble back ran for 246 of Wisconsin's 343 rushing yards with four touchdowns -- including a 54-yard scamper in the first quarter. Wisconsin went blow-for-blow with the Bruins' offense, as the Badgers gained nearly 500 yards of total offense on the afternoon.

The defense sacked McNown three times and recorded 10 tackles for loss on the day. Adamov recorded one sack and three tackles for loss, leading the team in the latter category. Doering's nine stops paced the rest of the Wisconsin defense, with Thompson right behind with seven. More importantly, they found themselves victors of one of the greatest upsets in Rose Bowl history. With five walk-on starters contributing, Wisconsin would celebrate a 38-31 win with another "Sea of Red" flowing through Pasadena.

The goal put forth early on that season came to fruition. The added sweat forged through stadium runs, the position drills, and the hill delivered a Big Ten and Rose Bowl championship squad.

"I'm proud of the coaches and players on that team" Adamov said. "There were five years' worth of guys, and none of us had the ring we saw the team get coming in as freshman back in '94. We didn't have a legacy going into that '98 season, but we finished with one. Coach Alvarez would always challenge the senior class on what stamp they were going to leave on the program. I think he's proud of the one that the '98 team left, and how the underclassmen were able to build on that the following season. I would like to think that team set a good example of what Wisconsin football was about."

The taste of victory was sweet, but it wouldn't be savored for long. Immediately after the game, Alvarez spoke to his players about moving forward.

"We were hootin' and hollerin' in the locker room for I don't know (how long)," Ferrario admitted, "and then Alvarez just dropped a bomb. 'We're celebrating tonight, we're celebrating tomorrow, but when we get back to Madison, you underclassmen – it's time to go back to work.'"

CHAPTER FOUR

Back-to-Back!

Wisconsin lost key contributors heading into the 1999 season. Gone were Tom Burke, Aaron Gibson, Cecil Martin, Mike Samuel and safety Leonard Taylor. Among the key former walk-ons departing included Adamov, Davenport and former walk-on tight end Eric Grams, who started in the Rose Bowl and caught nine passes for 100 yards on the season.

The team voted Thompson and McIntosh as captains for the second consecutive year. Dayne, Ghidorzi and Doering were also nominated to join them in leading the team.

There was also a special transition for a former walk-on between the seasons. Jason Eck was a reserve center who earned his scholarship before the 1997 season. The bonds between teammates are strong as they battled against each other on the field, but looked out for and protected each other off of it. Now, Eck was transitioning from being a player to a graduate assistant.

He had the intelligence for the coaching profession. As a senior, Eck made the 1998 Big-Ten Academic All-Conference Team, while also being named as Wisconsin's Athletic Board Scholar for Football. His linemen brothers highly respected his football IQ.

"We went to Jason many times just to go over plays," Ferrario said, who counts Eck as one of the most intelligent football players, outside of a quarterback, he has played with. "We'd be traveling and pull out the playbook, just asking him about assignments because he was the back-up center. 'At center, what are you looking at in this situation? What call would you make here?' He was a guy we definitely utilized a lot as a player."

Realizing he wouldn't supplant incumbent Casey Rabach at center, Eck decided after the Rose Bowl to graduate and focus on the LSAT tests for law school. According to Eck, Tauscher and some of his comrades in the trenches realized that life path wouldn't suit their former teammate, and so the night before the exam, his rambunctious group of loud friends purposely kept him up until the wee hours of the morning.

"I ended up sleeping through the LSAT," Eck said with a laugh, "which was the right decision."

He spoke with the coaches after the season, wanting to pursue a coaching career. Luckily, Jeff Wirth, the "White Rat" who transitioned from player to graduate assistant (GA) himself, planned to move on from Wisconsin. Eck interviewed for the vacant spot open on the staff and returned to UW as a GA.

The offensive linemen had to adjust to one of their more beloved teammates now becoming a coach. They would ask Eck to confirm practice schedules or other information only the coaches knew. Now working 10 to 15 hour days on the bottom rung of the coaching tree, Eck had to balance his friendships and his career aspirations, an odd and sometimes unfavorable position.

"I asked him, 'Are you going to be able to handle this now, because you cannot sit in the staff meeting and then go out and tell the guys on the team?' To his credit, he had a path that he wanted to follow," Hueber declared. "He was not unfriendly to those guys. I'm not going to tell you he never had a beer with them, but he was not going to give up what was said in the staff meetings about personnel. That is the true value of what he did. He came back and wanted to do it, and I thought it was good."

****

The Badgers would also have to find a new right tackle on the offensive line as the 6-foot-6, 375 pound Gibson was a first-round draft pick by the Detroit Lions in the 1999 NFL Draft.

Enter Tauscher. Spotted by a Wisconsin recruiter while playing prep basketball in Madison during the WIAA State Tournament in 1995, he was set to suit up for Division III Wisconsin-Stevens Point during his collegiate career. The Auburndale native instead walked on at UW and was a back-up to McIntosh at left tackle, but after that 1998 Rose Bowl season, even he was poised to move on from his days as a Badger.

The nimble and deceptively athletic tackle, who according to the 1998 media guide owned school records for left tackles in the vertical jump (27 inches) and the pro agility drill (4.73 seconds), couldn't get into Wisconsin's School of Education to work towards becoming a teacher. He earned his bachelor degree in history and was on the 1998 Wisconsin senior football poster. Tauscher had connections to Youngstown State, led by future Ohio State head coach Jim Tressel, and the university could help him reach the goal of becoming a teacher.

Not officially on the team and set to transfer, he didn't participate in the 1999 spring practices. With only a handful of credits to attend to during his spring semester at UW, he and Eck decided to travel whenever possible.

"There were a bunch of fun trips that spring. It was awesome," Tauscher laughed.

One of those fateful trips included a stop at the Kentucky Derby. There, the two former walk-ons ran into some of their former coaches, including Hueber. The chance opportunity allowed the two to discuss the tackle's future aspirations.

"The coaches seeing me and Jason down at the Derby allowed us to catch up. I think finding out what my plans were maybe refreshed their memories that I had a chance to come back to UW," Tauscher noted. "Obviously, we didn't get into great detail, but for me it was very fortunate timing. That is how I would describe it."

The encounter allowed for greater discussion down the road, and with his plans of heading to Division I-AA Youngstown State, Wisconsin realized he had an extra year of eligibility left.

"Here's the thing, and I became well versed in the graduate eligibility rules because of Tauscher," Hueber said. "Tauscher was maybe the first graduate transfer guy. He's going to graduate, and I'm saying goodbye to him, and the next thing we know, he can play for us, even if he graduates."

Hueber got on the telephone to his then-former lineman, hoping to reel him back to Madison and another season.

Mark Tauscher (68) takes a break during a 1999 practice. | Wisconsin State Journal

"So I called him and said, 'Would you think of coming back?' I'm the guy that screwed it up because I'm supposed to be on top of his eligibility. We weren't on top of it, now playing a fifth year is commonplace, but were weren't on top of that at the time.

"Let me say this, after going through that with Tauscher, we all were experts."

The coach told Tauscher there would be an opportunity to compete in replacing Gibson. Persuaded to come back to Wisconsin, he returned as a fifth-year senior, confident in his ability to show Hueber and new offensive coordinator Brian White he could play. In front of him was sophomore Brian Lamont, who appeared to be the frontrunner for first-team right tackle. It didn't take long for Tauscher to slide into that slot, however, as Lamont would deal with hamstring issues in camp. The career backup would take over his starting spot for the rest of the season. Having been a part of the offensive line previously, he adjusted to the line's communication seamlessly and was determined to not be a liability.

"I knew that I was the new guy," Tauscher said. "I had put in a lot of time. I spent a lot of time with those guys watching film. Even though I was able to get in and play in a lot of games, I had never been the starter. There was an adjustment. I wanted to make sure I wasn't going to be the weak link."

"When he got the opportunity, and this is a consistent theme for Tausch, he made the most of it," McIntosh said. "He improved throughout the season and ended up, I think, exceeding anybody's expectation in terms of what he could accomplish on the right side. He went from someone who we hoped could fill a void to excelling and being a NFL draft pick. Obviously, the rest is history as he capitalized on an opportunity his rookie year in Green Bay and never looked back."

****

After two dominating performances to start the 1999 season against Murray State and Ball State, the Badgers confidence was riding high. The next two games, however, would stunt their momentum.

UW traveled to face the Cincinnati Bearcats on September 18 in front of 27,000 fans. Statistically, Wisconsin overwhelmed their non-conference foe 425-261 in total yards. Dayne ran for 231 of UW's 340 rushing yards and a touchdown, and in the process broke former Ohio State running back Archie Griffin's all-time Big Ten rushing mark.

Costly mistakes and poor play from quarterback Scott Kavanagh, however, doomed the Badgers' chances at getting out of Ohio with a win. Dayne fumbled close to the Bearcats' goal line. A last-minute touchdown pass from Kavanagh to a young Lee Evans was called back by an illegal motion penalty. Wisconsin committed eight penalties, while Kavanagh completed only 8-of-21 passes in what would be a 17-12 upset. It's a defeat Tauscher and Thompson concede still pierces the emotions of those who played in that game.

The hard luck continued the following week facing No. 4 Michigan in the conference opener. Tom Brady again defeated the Badgers, throwing for 217 yards and two touchdowns. Dayne was held to a meager 88 yards on 22 carries, while Kavanagh again completed less than 50 percent of his passes.

Redshirt freshman Brooks Bollinger took over and would help draw UW within five points with under 90 seconds left in the game after his 13-yard touchdown run. The Badgers could not pull off the home victory, though, falling 21-16.

Now 2-2, the Badgers had to go to "The Horseshoe" to face the Buckeyes. Bollinger, who completed 6-of-9 passes against Michigan, would face national power Ohio State in his first career start.

It did not start well. By 10:23 in the second quarter, the Badgers were down 17-0. They went into the locker room down 17-6 after a pair of Vitaly Pisetsky field goals. A season once so hopeful was on the verge of collapse.

The locker room scene in Columbus, though, would be the turning point of the season. Tauscher recalled UW Director of Athletics Pat Richter reiterating how special the team was – something the former right tackle believed was powerful in regaining the team's confidence. Alvarez, who coached from the press box during the game because of a swollen right knee, came down and rallied his team. His words to the beleaguered squad ignited a self-fulfilling prophecy.

"Coach Alvarez comes in the locker room," Thompson recalled, "and to this day I don't know or understand how he had the confidence to do this, but he told us exactly how we were going to win. He came in and said, 'We're going down, we're going to cause a fumble on the opening kickoff, and the next play, we're going to give the ball to Ron and we're going to score – and we're going to come back and beat Ohio State.'"

Truer words were never spoken.

Michael Wiley took the second-half kickoff for the Buckeyes and was hit by Ryan Marks, forcing a fumble that was recovered by Wisconsin deep in OSU territory. Dayne scored his first of four second-half touchdowns on way to the Badgers racking up 42 unanswered points. Bollinger completed 15-of-27 passes on the day, the defense held OSU's offense to only 113 yards in the second half, and UW escaped Columbus with a 42-17 victory.

The Badgers wouldn't look back, reeling off a string of eight straight wins.

"I really don't know, but they remind me of that," Alvarez replied when asked about his halftime proclamation to his players. "It was something spontaneous. You don't think about those things. I never had anything planned on what to say although I knew I had to get their attention. You're at Ohio State. You're in a tough environment, you're behind but I sensed that we were a better team."

"He would do that throughout the course of the year," former nose tackle Eric Mahlik said. "He would tell us where we were going to be, and I think that we believed in his message so much that that's what would end up happening. He had such a great connection with the team, his players, and his coaches that his message was spot on."

****

Mahlik recorded two tackles in the Wisconsin win that turned the tide of the season. The Green Bay native was a consistent, full-time starter on the defensive line during the back-to-back championship years as well as the 2000 season. He was one of the few Badgers who went on to play in 50 games during his career.

An all-state selection from Green Bay Notre Dame high school, he bypassed a full ride from South Dakota and partial scholarships from Northern Iowa and Northern Michigan to head to Madison. Mahlik was undersized at 6-foot-3 and around 230 pounds. He was named team captain and MVP in his last prep season, but he admitted he wasn't much of a workout junkie during those years. That was something his new strength and conditioning coach would call him out on in his early days as a Badger.

"Those first few weeks we were training and doing things I had never done before in the weight room. I wasn't very strong to begin with," Mahlik admitted. "It was hard. I would equate it to boot camp in the military. They push you in order to expand your physical limits."

During a Friday workout session that included burnout lifts and circuit training, an intense Dettman made an example out of Mahlik. Calling him out in front of the team, it was a wake-up call for the prep standout.

Eric Mahlik (98) stops Michigan running back Anthony Thomas (32) for no gain. | AP Photo

The experience made him question staying in the program even though he just started.

"It was humiliating and humbling at the same time," Mahlik conceded. "It kind of made me realize that I had a long way to go to get where I wanted to be."

A fire lit beneath him, Mahlik dramatically improved his strength and was able to break through after that redshirt year with some upperclassmen exhausting their eligibility. He saw time in all 13 games during the 1997 season, then broke into the starting line-up, enhancing an already intimidating line boasting Burke, Kolodziej, Wendell Bryant and John Favret in 1998. He contributed 40 tackles, seven of them for loss, and five pass break-ups at the line of scrimmage.

Following up his second full season solidifying the defensive line, he earned defensive player of the week honors after a nine-tackle performance in a loss to the Wolverines. While he would go on to play another season, the scene in the locker room in Columbus was one he can still vividly recall to this day. The angst of a sizable deficit on the road, the frustration of players not executing for two-plus games, all turned around with a halftime declaration that would be a rallying cry for the rest of the season.

"We came out roaring in that second half," Mahlik said. "I can tell you the Horseshoe is one of the hardest places to play. The fans are loud. They're mean. It was probably one of the most memorable games of my career, to at least be a part of that, to make that comeback."

****

Alvarez would have knee replacement surgery at the Mayo Clinic in Minneapolis just days after the Ohio State game. He would watch his team's narrow 20-17 overtime victory against Minnesota from his hospital bed.

Another tough Purdue squad led by Brees gave the Badgers a battle, but ended with a 28-21 UW road win in West Lafayette on November 6. It was a game that Tauscher describes as a microcosm of the Badgers' season.

Doering led the defense with 17 tackles on the afternoon as the Boilermakers outgained UW in yardage (494 to 288) and first downs (34 to 14), but once again, Fletcher terrorized Brees with his second pick-six in as many years in the fourth quarter. The future NFL superstar threw for 350 yards, but three costly interceptions and Dayne's 222-yard performance secured a Wisconsin victory.

Seven days later, an electric atmosphere engulfed Camp Randall Stadium where 79,404 fans anticipated history. A Big Ten conference title was within grasp with Penn State losing to Michigan earlier that day. To up the ante further, Dayne was within 99 yards of Texas running back Ricky Williams' all-time rushing record set just one season earlier.

In the second quarter and the Badgers already up 20-3, Dayne broke off a 31-yard run in epic fashion, running down the field as frenzied fans cheered their all-time great into history. Pandemonium erupted from the stands and on the field.

"I just remember Coach Alvarez talking at the beginning of the year and how he made Ron's record such a team goal," Tauscher said. "I thought that was really smart of him because now everybody was part of it."

Dayne rushed for 216 yards and the Badgers cruised to 41-3 win over the Hawkeyes behind a defense led by Doering and Thompson, who recorded 10 and eight tackles, respectively.

With their season at one point in peril Wisconsin regrouped and captured an outright Big Ten Conference championship for the first time in 37 years. Finishing 9-2 overall and 7-1 in conference play, the championship gave them the chance to do something no other Big Ten team had ever done up to that point: win back-to-back Rose Bowls.

Many players recalled the different feel heading into the Rose Bowl game against Stanford compared with the previous season.

"Being an underdog many people thought we weren't even supposed to be there against UCLA," Doering said, "and then playing Stanford, we knew it was going to be a defensive battle. As a defensive player, you had to be ready. It was on us to win the game."

The Badgers started off sluggish in the first half, only scoring three points against a Cardinal defense that gave up 30 or more points in seven of its first 11 games. UW averaged over 35 points per game heading into the bowl game, but found themselves trailing 9-3 at halftime.

The Badgers started rolling in the second half. Dayne took a handoff and galloped 64 yards deep into Stanford territory. In that offset I-formation, Tauscher got just enough of Stanford linebacker Marc Stockbauer to help spring Dayne out into the open for the big gain. Later that drive, Dayne rumbled in from four yards out for the go-ahead touchdown and a 10-9 lead. UW wouldn't let go of that lead, and with a Bollinger touchdown run midway through the fourth quarter, the Badgers would reign once again in Pasadena.

Dayne gained 200 yards rushing to earn his second consecutive Rose Bowl MVP, and the defense held Stanford to -5 yards rushing in the game, 259 total. Thompson ended his UW career with nine tackles in his last game, tied for the team lead with Doering. The Badgers' secondary contained the explosive and consensus All-American Troy Walters, holding him to only three catches for 52 yards. With their 17-9 win, Wisconsin accomplished what no other Big Ten team had done in winning back-to-back Rose Bowl titles.

****

Once again, celebrations were abundant on the field. The Wisconsin marching band took to the field for the Fifth Quarter, but there was one celebratory act that may have gone unnoticed.

After the game, Ferrario looked around the swarm of players and coaches on the field and saw Tauscher, who a year earlier on the same field thought he had played his final game as a Badger. In his hand, a cigar was ready to be lit.

"I remember looking at him like, 'Where did that come

from?' number one," Ferrario reminisced with a laugh. "Number two, we're celebrating and going crazy after doing something no other Big Ten team has done before. I look over and I'm like, 'Can you even do that? Can you get in trouble for smoking a cigar down here?'"

When asked to confirm his fellow lineman's claims, the future NFL veteran didn't deny the daring feat.

"I have a great picture of having a cigar," Tauscher coyly admitted, though he wouldn't disclose the source of his tobacco contraband. "I don't know if it was lit, but I did have a cigar. I don't know if you can get away with that today, but yeah, we did find a way to get a cigar out there."

The high expectations coming into the season were nearly dashed by ten quarters of uncharacteristic play early on, but the Badgers were able to rally and racked up eight consecutive wins. They beat five ranked teams – the first time the program had ever accomplished that feat. This period of success for the Wisconsin program was highlighted by the emergence of Doering and Thompson, who were second and third, respectively, in tackles during the 1999 season. Doering and Mahlik both earned consensus All-Big Ten honorable mention selections.

The returning Tauscher started all 12 games. Not bad for a kid who came to Wisconsin still blocking with his forearms and not knowing what a "three-" or "five-technique" was. Dayne was obviously the highlight of the team, capping off his senior year by winning the Heisman Trophy, but the impact of the walk-ons' presence on that team has not been forgotten to this day.

"When you look around at the guys who contributed to those teams, we would be doing a disservice by ignoring the influence walk-ons had on the makeup of those teams," McIntosh stated. "I've talked to Coach Alvarez about this. He has referred to the development of the walk-ons in his program as the 'tipping point' – the playmakers – in his program. I don't know that you can have a start like we did in '99, and bounce back from it and run the table and be the only team to win back-to-back Rose Bowls without that type of contingency in your locker room."

"It was that commitment and that willingness to go above and beyond which really separated those teams," Thompson said.

"Very selfishly, I tell you – I think those were really the best teams in Wisconsin history."

CHAPTER FIVE

From Paying to Play to Getting Paid: UW Walk-Ons in the NFL

Players from the back-to-back Rose Bowl teams not only delivered in the college game, many went on to respectable careers in the NFL. Thirty former Badgers – including six former walk-ons – found themselves on NFL rosters.

Since 1990, 18 former UW walk-ons have made the journey from unknown recruit to being on a 53-man, NFL roster.

From that list of 18, four played at least a decade. Two have earned the right to play in Hawaii as Pro Bowl honorees, while Mark Tauscher and Chris Maragos have helped their teams capture the Lombardi Trophy as Super Bowl champions. One former walk-on currently residing in Houston dominates opposing offensive lines as the best defensive player in the game today.

NFL teams have drafted nine Wisconsin walk-ons since 1990. Nebraska, the model Alvarez based his vision upon, has had eleven in that same timeframe according to an April 2016 article by the *Omaha World-Herald*.

Jason Doering captained the 2000 squad before the Indianapolis Colts picked him with the 193rd overall pick in the 2001 draft. The sixth-round selection would play four

Jason Doering (34) was a 6th round selection of the Indianapolis Colts. | AP Photo

seasons from 2001-04 between the Indianapolis Colts and the Washington Redskins. He played 53 games with seven starts and 91 career tackles, including a career-high 12 tackles (11 solo) as a starter in the Colts' 40-21 loss to San Francisco on November 25, 2001.

A year earlier, Mark Tauscher found a NFL home just up the road from Madison. The last Wisconsin player selected in the 2000 draft, the offensive tackle would be a seventh round pick, the 224th player taken by the Green Bay Packers and general manager Ron Wolf. Tauscher would go on to play 11 years in the league.

"There's a lot of angst because you think you're going to go in a certain place, and sitting there you realize at any moment a phone call's going to change the entire direction of your life," Tauscher explained. "To get that call was a huge relief. That part of it, just getting drafted, settles in. Then the idea of 'Man, I get a chance to go to Green Bay,' which is a team that I grew up watching. It was pretty exciting."

Late round draft picks are never locks to make a team's roster and most have an uphill battle to climb. It's comparable to being a walk-on in the sense of proving oneself over again, with a roster spot and your professional career on the line. Tauscher not only made the Green Bay roster, he proceeded to play 134 games from 2000-2010, including 132 starts. Where many had failed, what were the keys to a long, prosperous career?

"Well, I think anytime you are drafted in the NFL, does the system fit and are you able to stay healthy? Are you able to take advantage of the opportunities you get?" Tauscher said. "As a late pick, if you have a bad training camp your first year, you're more than likely going to be bouncing around for a while. I was fortunate that I got a great opportunity early with a couple of guys getting injured and being able to showcase that I could play. A lot of guys don't get that chance, and there are guys entrenched in spots.

"The big thing for me was always earn the coaches' trust – show them that you're going to be able to do what they're asking of you. Not just being on time for meetings and being prepared with the playbook, but being available and making sure the coaches trust you. That was always my goal. I wanted to make sure I didn't have any mental errors, and you try to put yourself in a position to be successful. That's kind of what I tried to do during my 11 years: make sure you're available and you can be accountable for what you're doing."

Tauscher earned that trust and praise during his first summer camp, resulting in plenty of reps on the field. With a back injury limiting incumbent Earl Dotson, Tauscher slid in at right tackle during the preseason. He took over the position for good in Green Bay's second game of the season against Buffalo.

His first career start came the week after against the Philadelphia Eagles on September 17, a 6-3 win. Tauscher and 2000 second-round draft pick Chad Clifton would form a duo that held both tackle spots on the offensive line into the 2011 season. They combined to start 292 games, protecting two of the three legendary quarterbacks in franchise history, Brett Favre and Aaron Rodgers.

Tauscher played a part in some of the Packers most memorable games. When asked about highlights from his time in Green Bay, the December 22, 2003 game at Oakland instantly jumped into his head. Favre, just one day removed from his father's death, completed 22 of 30 passes for 399 yards and four touchdowns in an emotional 41-7 victory.

Tauscher also recalled the back-breaking loss to the Philadelphia Eagles in the NFC Divisional playoff game later that season, better known to many Packers faithful as the infamous "4th-and-26" contest. Philadelphia quarterback Donovan McNabb connected with receiver Freddie Mitchell on a fourth down play that required 26 yards, setting up a game-tying field goal to send it to overtime where the Eagles

Right tackle Mark Tauscher (65) played 11 years for the Green Bay Packers. | AP Photo

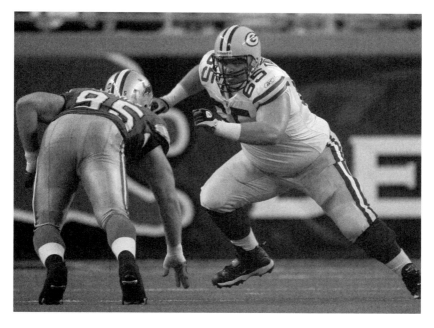

won 20-17. Tauscher said that loss, which would have propelled Green Bay to the conference championship game, still stings.

His last few seasons were injury-plagued, as he played in just 25 games his last three seasons in the league. He was placed on injured reserve (IR) in December 2008 for a torn ACL, then re-signed with the Packers and played eight games in 2009.

After signing a deal in March 2010, Tauscher started the first four games of the season before he suffered a shoulder injury against the Detroit Lions. He would be placed on IR yet again, and it would be the last time he would technically suit up for the Green and Gold. However, he'd bear witness to one of the greatest hot streaks an NFL franchise has experienced that culminated with a Super Bowl XLV victory over the Pittsburgh Steelers. It was a daunting season, as the team at one point was 8-6 with their star quarterback injured and on the outside looking in for a spot in the playoffs. Two final regular season wins, then four straight playoff victories as the NFC's sixth seed led them back to the Lombardi Trophy.

"That team was resilient," Tauscher stated. "There were a lot of injuries, myself included. I don't exactly remember how many guys were on IR, but that's really where Aaron and Jordy and that whole young group kind of took over. It just goes to show you that even though things look down you're never out of it in the NFL. You get hot and play with a ton of confidence, and play well when you need to."

The Packers released Tauscher in late July 2011. He retired, but has definitely stayed busy since, with football still a big part of his life. He's worked in the booth with Matt Lepay and Mike Lucas as one of the two color commentators calling Wisconsin home football games and covered the Packers as a pregame and postgame analyst for 620 WTMJ in Milwaukee. He formed a radio show on WTMJ with good friend and fullback John Kuhn for a couple of seasons, and will debut a daily show on the ESPN Wisconsin radio network with ESPN writer Jason Wilde in August 2016.

Outside of football, he has taken a number of opportunities presented to him and made them a success. He's been involved with American Family Children's Hospital in Madison on its Development Partners Advisory Board, as well as the UW School of Education's Board of Visitors. He joined Red Card in the summer of 2014, a company that has developed an off-campus meal plan for UW-Madison students. The leadership team for Red Card, Jeff Haupt and Craig Bartlett, also combined forces with Tauscher to buy the Madison newspaper and website *Isthmus* in July 2014.

He's found success on and off the field, and the time spent at Wisconsin helped shape his approach to his many endeavors.

"With walk-ons, and for everybody in general, it's always good when you earn something. You kind of have to prove to yourself that you belong – whether you're a scholarship player or not. I think that those things are always good," Tauscher said. "If you continue to work at something and you put in the time, you can get opportunities. I think that's the key for walk-ons at UW – you're going to get an opportunity. Are you going to be prepared for it when it comes? "

****

Six years before Tauscher, Joe Panos was able to savor a Rose Bowl victory then make his way to play in the East-West Shrine game. He and fullback Mark Montgomery were the only Badgers selected in the 1994 draft, and both were drafted by the Philadelphia Eagles. The Eagles hoped to shore up their offensive line and that included picking up Panos in the third round with the 77th overall pick, while Montgomery would be drafted in the seventh. Ironically, Philadelphia also drafted Goodwin – the UCLA safety that was ejected with Montgomery in the Rose Bowl – in the fifth round.

It would be the beginning of 54 games played in the "City

of Brotherly Love" for the former Badgers lineman, which included 40 starts in four seasons. He would later sign with the Buffalo Bills in 1998, starting all 16 games that season. A neck injury forced him out for all of 1999, but he returned for 13 games in 2000. After a brief stay with the New

Joe Panos (72) was the 77th overall pick in the 1994 NFL draft. | AP Photo

England Patriots in 2001, Panos retired in the first week of training camp.

Panos still has a hand in the game. He's a certified contract advisor for Athletes First, one of the premiere player agencies in the nation. The former All-American also kept his ties to Wisconsin, as he represents a slew of former Badgers including Travis Frederick, Rob Havenstein and Schobert. He also is the agent for Rick Wagner, another former UW walk-on.

****

The Baltimore Ravens selected Wagner in the fifth round of the 2013 draft. Some mock drafts prior to the 2012 season, however, had Wagner going much higher. Fox Sports' Peter Schrager picked him to go No. 13 to the Cincinnati Bengals from his April 30, 2012 article, while ESPN's Todd McShay noted he had the All-Big Ten honoree going No. 2 overall in his early mock draft.

It didn't work out that way, as 167 players heard their names called before him. He started 13 games his senior year, missing one due to a right knee injury. Though it appears his draft stock fell, he was picked up by head coach John Harbaugh and general manager Ozzie Newsome 35 picks into the fifth round. Joining Wisconsin in 2008 as an unheralded tight end but finishing as a team captain, he approached his new journey into professional football in the same manner.

"I think it's kind of a similar situation as being a walk-on in college," Wagner admitted during 2015 training camp. "I was drafted in the lower rounds, so I kind of had to prove myself to the team that I do belong here. I can make a NFL roster."

His entrance to the league was a baptism by fire, as starting right tackle Michael Oher went down with an ankle injury against the Denver Broncos and Wagner was thrown into action in his first-ever NFL game. Veteran outside linebacker Shaun Phillips introduced the Wisconsin native to the big leagues, as the Broncos defender recorded two-and-a-half sacks in Denver's 49-27 victory.

Wagner would continue to improve, however, to the point where the organization allowed Oher to leave for the Tennessee Titans in free agency. Heading into the 2016 season, the Wisconsin product has played in 47 of 48 career regular season games, including starting 31 of the last 32 at right tackle for the Ravens. In 2014, he was rated as the top right tackle by Pro Football Focus.

2015 would bring injuries to his knee and ankle, but he started all 16 games. He's a key asset on the right side of the offensive line, and has had the approval and respect of his head coach for the past few seasons.

"When a player takes what he's learned in practice into the game, that's really encouraging. Because we were really happy with what Rick was doing in practice," Ravens head coach John Harbaugh said after the Ravens' August 7, 2014 preseason game against the 49ers. "I think someone wrote it earlier, you don't notice him much. That's a good thing for a right tackle, and he seemed like he played that way. And at the end of the day, he was solid and on his targets, and his footwork was good. He's a good, solid football player."

Prior to playing on Sundays, or even piling up his all-conference honors in Madison, Wagner's priority in high school was basketball. He played on an AAU team but started focusing more on football his junior year of high school. He excelled at tight end at West Allis Hale. He caught 39 passes for an astounding 900 yards and six touchdowns in his career for Hale head coach Scott Otto, utilizing his tall frame and basketball rebounding skills to his advantage.

Wagner accepted the preferred walk-on opportunity offered by Wisconsin offensive line coach Bob Bostad despite

Ricky Wagner (71) continues to be a mainstay on the Ravens offensive line. | AP Photo

Division I basketball offers from UW-Green Bay, UW-Milwaukee, and a couple of football offers. He joined fellow future starter Bradie Ewing as walk-ons in the class of 2008 which included key contributors like Shelton Johnson, Marcus Cromartie, Brad Nortman, Peter Konz and Kevin Zeitler. All ended up playing on Sundays in the NFL.

He was listed as a tight end when coming to UW, but that wouldn't last a season. Wagner's agility caught the eye of Dettman while the freshman was performing overhead squats one day. For offensive linemen, coaches look at how each player bends. If they naturally bend with their knees rather than at their waist, it's a promising sign that they display good balance to help ward off opposing rushers. The former hardwood standout showed the ability to bend and Dettman shared his observations with the coaching staff. The writing was on the wall for the position change.

"I think they knew they would move me to 'O-line' pretty quickly, but I kind of held on to the dream of being a tight end," Wagner laughed when recalling his early time at Wisconsin. "But that didn't work out."

"We just thought he was a really good athlete," said Rudolph, then the tight ends coach at UW. "He was a good basketball player, played tight end and when he got here, he kept growing. He was 6-foot-6 and weighed 245 (pounds) when he showed up in the summer. By the end of summer, he was 260, and by the second week of camp, he was 270, and that's when we moved him over. He did a great job, and Bob (Bostad) did a great job with him."

Known to be demanding, the UW offensive line coach had a stable of future NFL prospects starting on the line in left tackle Gabe Carimi, guard-center John Moffitt and guard Kraig Urbik. Wagner would redshirt that year, officially moving to the offensive line early in the season. It would be a daunting process, but one that could be done with the coaching staff in place and the caliber of players in front of him.

"Gaining the weight really wasn't difficult for me. I feel like I was going that way anyways with my development," said Wagner. "The change of position, just the coaching staff and the guys around me made it much easier than maybe somewhere else. Coach Bostad believed in me from the beginning. He was definitely a tough coach to play for, but he really helped out everybody. It seemed like everybody went to the NFL who I played with. (I was) just trying to do what they do every day, and watching how they played the position."

After that redshirt season, Wagner played in 12 of UW's 13 games in 2009 as a back-up to Carimi at left tackle. He would get his shot on the right side of the line the next season as a knee injury forced former five-star tackle Josh Oglesby out of the game against San Diego State. Even before subbing in for the former high school prodigy, the walk-on was pushing for reps early that season. He solidified an offensive line that opened holes for the likes of John Clay, James White and Montee Ball all the way to Pasadena.

UW ran for 245.7 yards per game, good for 12th in the nation. They built a wall of protection around quarterback Scott Tolzien, allowing only 14 sacks on the season. Wagner would earn an all-conference honorable mention selection for his efforts, starting 10 of the final 11 games just two years removed from the position change.

Carimi would go on to the NFL after UW's heartbreaking 21-19 loss to TCU in the 2011 Rose Bowl. He was selected in the first round by the Chicago Bears, and the coaching staff would ask Wagner to take over for the Outland Trophy winner.

The left side of the offensive line is known as the "blind side" for right-handed quarterbacks, as the signal callers do not see defenders facing that side when they receive the snap and begin to drop back. Left tackles need to be agile and athletic enough to halt the momentum of the opposing team's pass rushers. That duty would now be bestowed upon the West Allis native, but the continuity and reps accumulated helped make for a seamless transition.

With the addition of N.C. State transfer quarterback Russell Wilson for the 2011 season, Wisconsin's offense

WALK-ON THIS WAY

evolved even further into a potent threat. Ball rushed for
1,923 yards and a conference record 33 touchdowns, as the
team ranked 10th in the nation with 237.4 yards per contest.
Offensive coordinator Paul Chryst's offense could do no
wrong at times, as they scored 44.6 points per game, fourth-
best in the FBS. Wagner started all 14 games at left tackle,
recording 67 knockdowns and 11 touchdown-resulting blocks
earning him an All-Big Ten honorable mention selection
again.

Hopes were high for the now-former walk-on, who earned
a scholarship early in the 2010 season. In addition to the
way-too-early mock draft predictions, Wagner would also be
named a *Sports Illustrated* preseason first-team All-
American. Despite the rough 8-6 season that included a
position coach change two games into the 2012 season, he
earned a seat as a team captain on way to first-team all-
conference honors, as well as being named a second-team
All-American selection by CBSSports.com.

Currently, he's looking forward to the new season ahead of
him after having a series of nagging injuries last year. The
tested tackle will look to anchor the Ravens' offensive line
with a performance similar to 2014. He's been used to
proving himself time after time.

"(Being a walk-on) really prepared me for my professional
career. You have to prove it over and over again just like I did
in my college career."

****

Defensive lineman J.J. Watt spoke with the media shortly
after being selected by the Houston Texans with the No. 11
pick in the 2011 draft. Questions ranged from his knowledge
of Wade Phillips' defense and how he would be used within
it, to whether he had spoken with former Badgers Owen
Daniels and Garrett Graham. Both former UW tight ends
played for head coach Gary Kubiak in Houston.

One reporter asked the Pewaukee native what his greatest
strength was. Watt could have noted his large frame. At 6-

foot-5 and hovering between 285-290 pounds, he recorded 14 passes defended and blocked four kicks in his career at Wisconsin. Or it could have been his intelligence, as he was a two-time Academic All-Big Ten honoree in 2009 and 2010. His answer, however, shouldn't have been much of a surprise to anyone, especially those close to him.

"My biggest strength is my work ethic," Watt declared. "I am going to put a ton of time in the film room, weight room, and on the field. I am going to give you every single thing I have, every single play, and at the end of the day we're going to win football games because of it."

There's an edge that drives most walk-ons to the success they see on the field. Watt thrives on his uncanny drive for excellence, as that "Dream Big, Work Hard" attitude has helped him jump from unheralded recruit to one of the NFL's greatest defensive linemen.

That work ethic started early. When asked about his work ethic during that same conference call, he attributed the mentality from lessons instilled by his parents, John and Connie. It showed during his high school years, especially when training for football. Brad Arnett, the owner and director of sports performance at NX Level, has trained Watt since his sophomore year in high school. He's seen first-hand the development of the league's most feared defender.

"You get a feel for work-ethic and attention to detail, their character and how bad they want it. He met all of those," said Arnett, who's also worked in both the University of Arizona and University of Minnesota's strength and conditioning programs. "There was never a question with his work ethic. He always busted his ass. He always wanted to be good. It was his goal."

One winter morning in particular, a snowstorm blanketed the state with blizzard-like conditions. Arnett, who had been working out with Watt at 5:30 in the morning three times a week, didn't think the kid would call and show up in the midst of the terrible winter conditions.

Then a call came at about five o'clock.

"'Coach, you're still going to be there, right?'" Arnett

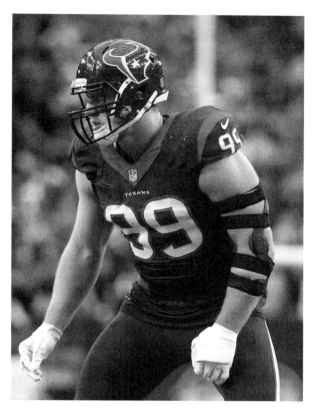

JJ Watt (99) has become the most dominant defensive player in the NFL today. | AP Photo

recalled Watt asking.

"'Yup, I'll be there.'"

"We're in a middle of a snowstorm and he pulls up. This is in the days when you don't turn the heat on until you're in there. We're going through warm-ups with winter coats on and you can see your breath, but he was always consistently there, always pushing himself.'"

Watt's development fits the description of what Alvarez would call a late bloomer. Arnett remembered the former hockey standout was tall but came in just over 200 pounds. Some college coaching staffs wondered if he'd ever fill out his frame. In a similar fashion to Alvarez, Arnett based his analysis on a player's hands, wrists, ankles and feet. His athletic training staff administered a body composition test to Watt. His wrist measurement, which denotes an athlete's bone density, was "off the charts." The future All-Pro had a chance if he worked at it. According to Arnett, Watt filled out to around 250 pounds at the time of his verbal commitment.

Despite building that frame, a setback in the form of mononucleosis halted chances of attending summer camps between his junior and senior season. That limited his opportunities in front of the Wisconsin coaching staff.

In Bret Bielema's time as head coach, the staff would like to have recruits participate in their camps before receiving offers. Watt would, however, pick up scholarship offers from Minnesota, Central Michigan and Colorado and made the decision to commit to the Chippewas. As often happens in college football, changes to coaching staffs can make one rethink their initial verbal pledge.

"Brian Kelly was the head coach at Central Michigan, and he left to go to Cincinnati. Butch Jones took over there, but J.J. didn't know Jones real well," said Clay Iverson, Watt's head coach at Pewaukee. "He liked Glen Mason at Minnesota, and Minnesota offered him after Central, but J.J. didn't want to break his commitment, and he did like Kelly. When that kind of went down, things kind of blew up."

The two-star prospect's recruiting wouldn't end there, however. Iverson was in Eau Claire when he watched the Gophers blow a 31-point lead to Texas Tech in the Insight Bowl. Winds of change would come that would force Watt's hand again to make a change in schools.

"As I'm watching the Gophers lose to Tech, I'm thinking this might not be good.'" Iverson said. "Glen Mason was fired the next day. Because J.J. had de-committed after Kelly left Central Michigan and committed to the Gophers, we said we would keep our commitment and went to Minnesota for a visit. Things didn't go well with the new Gopher coach Tim Brewster. J.J. came back and said he didn't have a good feeling about this. I said, 'That's okay, we can start the process all over again.'"

Butch Jones came back into the picture, and Watt flipped back to the Chippewas. He would head to Central Michigan as a tight end after catching 38 passes for 549 yards and 11 touchdowns at Pewaukee. Watt would earn first-team all-state and all-conference honors as both a tight end and defensive end in his senior season. Like many prep athletes, he participated in multiple sports, becoming state champion in the shot put his final year while also lettering in basketball and baseball. Before his school days were over, the *Milwaukee Journal Sentinel* named him their prep sports Male Athlete of the Year.

In Central Michigan's spread offense, Watt played in all 14 games his true freshman season. Despite catching eight passes for 77 yards for the Midwestern Athletic Conference (MAC) champions that year, he wasn't necessarily where he wanted to be. Iverson recalled speaking with Watt a couple of times during that 2007 season. He knew his former player well enough to know he wasn't happy.

His father, John, remembers his first game against Kansas that J.J. only played about 15 snaps as a tight end. J.J. wanted to be more involved, but Jones' offense didn't feature the tight end prominently. According to John, both J.J. and another Chippewa tight end were going to be moved to offensive tackle the following year.

Arnett recalled he and J.J. discussing the possibility of coming back home to not just walk-on to Wisconsin, but to switch over to the defensive side of the ball. In that conversation, Watt wanted his trainer's opinion about making the bold jump.

"'First of all, you need to sit down and have a serious conversation with Mom and Dad because UW is not going to scholarship you,'" Arnett remembered saying to his pupil. "You're going to have to walk-on. But if you're asking me do I think you can do it? Absolutely."

Bielema and Watt connected, and the opportunity to walk-on presented itself. Watt trained at NX Level with Arnett a few days a week while also taking classes at a local community college in the spring. He also worked at the Pizza Hut in town.

Watt moved to defensive end at UW, and his dedication to learning the craft was evident. Sitting out as his redshirt year due to NCAA transfer regulations would allow him to dissect his new assignments and techniques. It would also allow him to go against future NFL talents Carimi, Moffitt and Urbik.

"We recruited J.J. out of high school," conceded Bielema, "but he was obviously a lot smaller. He was a late bloomer. I remember his visit like it was yesterday. He was really excited. He asked what he had to do to get a scholarship. I said he had to put himself in a role that showed him as a first or second string player that would help us win a Big Ten championship. And he said, 'I'll have a scholarship by the end of the spring.'"

"And that's exactly what he did. He earned it his first spring there."

That was on the field. Off the field defensive line coach Charlie Partridge remembered Watt approaching him after practice asking him to watch film of his scout team practices. The newly minted position coach didn't get a chance to work hands on with Watt during practice, as he was preparing the first- and second-team linemen for each week's opponents. But Watt wanted guidance and coaching, so they watched film of his work on the scout team.

The hype continued building for the next season. A *Milwaukee Journal Sentinel* article from December 2008 noted how Watt might have been in the two-deep of the depth chart based on his brief but dramatic ascension at end. The hard work was paying off for the walk-on.

"He was working to get better every day," Partridge said, now entering his third season as head coach at Florida Atlantic University. "It didn't take too long, once we got into spring after that fall he had to show that he was going to be a major contributor immediately. By the end of spring, he had become a force, and one that a scholarship was imminent."

Watt earned a scholarship starting for the fall of 2009, and combined with senior O'Brien Schofield to form an impressive duo of defensive ends. He started all 13 games of that 10-3 season for the Badgers. He accumulated 15.5 tackles for loss and 4.5 sacks, placing him second and third on the team in those categories, respectively. That would earn him All-Big Ten honorable mention honors by the media.

2010 would be the true breakout season for him, and the hype machine was in full effect. The Lott IMPACT Trophy Award, Bronko Nagurski Trophy and Bednarik Award committees all named him to their watch lists. The stage was set for a big season, and the Badgers would be tested during that 13-game schedule. A clutch player thrives on the biggest stages and in the most critical of times. In three particular contests, Watt delivered.

The first would be under the lights of Camp Randall Stadium on October 16, when Wisconsin faced No. 1 Ohio State. Against the perennial powerhouse and conference rival, he'd sack quarterback Terrelle Pryor twice – including an 11-yard loss on the Buckeyes' last drive – in UW's 31-18 upset win.

The following week at Iowa his sack may have been the most important of the season for Bielema's squad. The Badgers picked up the go-ahead touchdown on Ball's eight-yard run with 1:06 left in the game. The defense would have to hold a 31-30 lead against the Hawkeyes' offense led by quarterback Ricky Stanzi. In four plays, Iowa drove to the Wisconsin's 49-yard line, and momentum was gathering for the home team to get within field goal range for a potential-game winning attempt. Watt, who had already recorded a tackle for a loss and blocked an extra point attempt earlier in the game, would need to step up yet again.

"We had a conversation quickly on the sideline. I said, 'You might have to get out of your gap and take a risk,'" Partridge recalled. "He did it, and ended up sacking the quarterback to essentially end the drive."

Watt would sack Stanzi back at the Iowa 38, causing an 11-yard loss and head coach Kirk Ferentz to call one of his timeouts. Four plays later, linebacker Mike Taylor would tackle running back Adam Robinson in bounds at the Wisconsin 35-yard line, causing the game clock to run out and the Badgers smelling a potential Rose Bowl berth.

"You can't do that with all players, but when you have someone like him – really the better they are the more risk you can take," Partridge continued. "It worked out pretty good a number of times."

Watt may have saved his best for his last regular season game as a college player.

He was named Big Ten Defensive Player of the Week after a monstrous game, recording seven tackles (three for loss), one sack, and forcing two fumbles in a 70-23 stomping of Northwestern. He added another extra point block and three quarterback hurries – all of which contributed to UW interceptions. In front of 80,011 rabid Badgers fans longing for the first Rose Bowl berth in 11 years, Wisconsin sealed the deal to head back to Pasadena.

"I remember he took a long time to go off the field," Jeff Potrykus of the *Milwaukee Journal Sentinel's* said. "You could tell he was really soaking it in that day because he knew in his mind that that was it. There wasn't going to be another game at Camp Randall for him."

There would be the heartbreak of a 21-19 Rose Bowl loss to TCU on January 1, 2011, one that left Watt sobbing in postgame press conference. His 2010 season would go down in school history as one of the finest seasons a Wisconsin defensive player has ever recorded. He led the team with seven sacks, 21 tackles for loss, and three blocked kicks.

For his efforts, Watt won the Lott IMPACT Trophy award, which honors "College Football's defensive best in character and performance." He also earned first-team All-American honors by *Pro Football Weekly,* second-team by both the Associated Press and *Sports Illustrated*. He was also a consensus first-team All-Big Ten selection.

Making a tough decision, Watt declared for the NFL Draft. Rated as a first round pick he accepted the invite from the NFL to come out to New York for the draft. He invited his family, along with Iverson and another high school assistant, to Radio City Music Hall.

Nervousness and excitement surrounded not just the Watts, but all of the kids in the green room.

"It was just a general feeling in the room," John Watt said, who admitted he had to introduce himself to Alabama head coach Nick Saban during the evening. "Here we are back in this room with 20 some young men, the tension is so thick you could cut it with a knife."

According to Iverson, there were some rumors about Watt going in the top ten selections, but those cooled after the Jacksonville Jaguars drafted Missouri quarterback Blaine Gabbert with the tenth overall pick. Others placed him in the mid to late first round range. The current Mukwonago high school football coach remembered Watt stepping away from the table to speak with Gabbert, the second quarterback to be selected in the draft.

"His cell phone rings and his younger brother, T.J., picks it up, who's a sophomore (in high school) at the time," Iverson recalled with a laugh. "I don't think I've ever seen someone get a phone ripped out of his hands quicker."

That wouldn't be *the* phone call, though. With the Houston Texans picking next Kubiak and defensive coordinator Wade Phillips surprised Watt, taking him with the eleventh overall pick in the first round.

"When he stood up and they handed him that Texans hat and he put it on, how could you not be proud as a father and as a family?" John Watt said. "It's what the kids have worked so hard for. It is everything everybody says it is. It's unbelievable, it's surreal. Your son just went from being a hardworking teenager essentially, to somebody who's now in the professional ranks, and in one phone call is a multi-millionaire."

Watt found modest success his rookie year. Starting in all 16 games, he tallied 56 tackles with 4.5 sacks in the regular season. The biggest impact came from his clutch play, something that has been recognized throughout his relatively short career. During the January 7, 2012 Wild Card playoff game against the Cincinnati Bengals, Watt's coming out party to the NFL was in full force.

Playing against former TCU quarterback Andy Dalton, who beat Watt and Wisconsin just a year and six days earlier in the 2011 Rose Bowl, the Texans rookie intercepted a pass in the second quarter. Showcasing his tremendous athleticism, he returned it 29 yards for a touchdown. His efforts led to a 31-10 victory over Dalton and the Bengals. He finished that post-season with 3.5 sacks, a launching point to what many say is one of the most dominant defensive performances in recent years.

Before the 2012 season, the buzz around Watt's second season was deafening. Phillips highly touted his defensive end in interviews to the media, even going so far as to predict Watt would have a bust in the Pro Football Hall of Fame.

Since then, Watt hasn't disappointed, taking his game to the next level, and then some. Consider the past four years for the former walk-on:

2012: 81 tackles, 20.5 sacks (led the league, 9th player in league history to register 20-plus sacks), 16 passes defended (league record for defensive linemen)

2013: 80 tackles, 10.5 sacks, seven passes defended

2014: 78 tackles, 20.5 sacks (the first person to ever record multiple 20-sack seasons in a career), 10 passes defended, *five touchdowns*

2015: 76 tackles, 17.5 sacks, eight passes defended

To say Watt has been a dominant force is an understatement. He won the AP Defensive Player of the Year three times in five seasons. He's been a four-time AP All-Pro, as well as a four-time Pro Bowl selection. In 2014, he was even used on offense, catching three touchdown passes in red zone opportunities. He also had an 80-yard interception return for a touchdown, recovered a fumble for another score, and was credited with a safety giving him 32 points scored that season. *As a defensive end.*

As his game's evolved on the field, it can be traced back to that work ethic that started back in the Waukesha area as a teenager.

Watt has had to pump the breaks early on heading into the 2016 offseason, however, as an affliction of injuries finally took its toll on the NFL's version of Superman. A broken hand, a sports hernia, groin tears and a herniated disc finally made him succumb and he came out of the AFC

Wild Card Playoff game in January.

"During the season, he would never say anything, and obviously when he broke his hand, he called and let us know he would have to wear the club and that was going to affect his play," John said. "As far as his other injuries, he's pretty tight lipped about all that kind of stuff at least during the season. He did admit to us after the season was over and he was going through his surgeries and everything that this was by far his most difficult season injury-wise."

ESPN's Tania Ganguli reported in late March that there were five tears in his core, upper legs and groin area. Speaking with MMQB.com's Peter King in an April 2016 article, Watt admitted the surgery on January 12 went about 90 minutes longer than projected. He would need to step away from training and physical activity for five weeks, but gradually, he would work his way back.

"When I was in Philadelphia after the first surgery, there were some days there where I really questioned whether or not I'd ever be able to play again," Watt conceded to reporters during a September 7, 2016 press conference. "Just some of the stuff we were dealing with from a rehab standpoint, and just the way that the recovery was going early on – but that was way back in January and February. There was a very low point there."

Watt's drive and energy has helped him into a leadership role with his teammates. He bought a cabin in Waukesha County that serves as his offseason home and training facility. In March 2016, he invited some of his teammates up to Wisconsin for a week of offseason conditioning and work. According to Arnett, 25 came to the Badger State to work and to bond.

"Every single one of them matches what he does," Arnett said. "What was kind of neat for me was to sit back and watch the dialogue, whether it was here or at his house doing a cornhole tournament. Because he's considered the best of the best, he's grown into the role where he is leader. Guys are looking up to him and watching what he does because they've seen what he puts into it. They want to meet that expectation. The guys that accept that, and are okay with it, get better."

There's also the generous side to Watt. According to his father, J.J. and his mom, Connie, worked with the UW law department when he was a junior at UW to start the Justin J. Watt Foundation. The organization reaches out to schools across the nation that don't have the funds for after-school athletic programs. Since 2011, the foundation's donated over $2 million to schools. His charity softball competitions have been a hit. The most recent in May 2016 drew over 30,000 people at Minute Maid Park in Houston, and had former first lady Barbara Bush throw out the first pitch. That event alone raised over $2 million.

The sky's the limit for the Wisconsin walk-on. There's no doubt Watt, who now has his own logo thanks to a

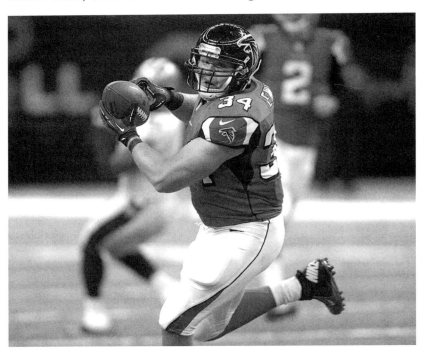

Bradie Ewing (34) was drafted in the 5th round by the Atlanta Falcons in 2012. | AP Photo

sponsorship deal with Reebok, will jump back from his injuries to wreak havoc on opposing offenses for years to come. If there's any indication based on the precedent he's already set his first five years in the league, his sixth will continue a legacy that could land him immortalized in Canton.

Wisconsin Walk-Ons Who Have Been Selected in the NFL Draft From 1990-2016

1994
Joe Panos – Philadelphia Eagles (3rd round, 77th overall pick)
2000
Mark Tauscher – Green Bay Packers (7th round, 224th overall pick)
2001
Jason Doering – Indianapolis Colts (6th round, 193rd overall pick)
2008
Paul Hubbard – Cleveland Browns (6th round, 191st overall pick)
2011
J.J. Watt – Houston Texans (1st round, 11th overall pick)

2012
Bradie Ewing – Atlanta Falcons (5th round, 157th overall pick)
2013
Rick Wagner – Baltimore Ravens (5th round, 168th overall pick)
2014
Jared Abbrederis – Green Bay Packers (5th round, 176th overall pick)
2016
Joe Schobert – Cleveland Browns (4th round, 99th overall pick)

****

Both Paul Hubbard (89) and Joe Schobert (53) were picked up by the Cleveland Browns. Hubbard was a 6th round draft pick in 2008. Schobert was the 99th overall pick in the 2016 NFL draft. | AP Photo

From 1990 to 2016, nine other walk-ons made it to the NFL as undrafted free agents. They weren't highly sought after, overlooked for some measurement or intangible pro scouts didn't see translating to the professional game. Many, once again, would have that chip on their shoulders to prove the doubters wrong.

"It was very similar to my walk-on experience," said Donnel Thompson, who played for the Pittsburgh Steelers and Indianapolis Colts from 2000-02. "I was pissed I wasn't drafted. I got a chance to see some of the other guys that were drafted and other guys that were free agents, and I knew I could compete with them. I was going to get to practice early, and I was going to stay late. At night I was going to make sure I studied."

After the 2000 Rose Bowl, Thompson would begin his professional football journey. He blocked a field goal to force a tie in the 2000 Hula Bowl, an all-star game featuring some of the nation's best collegiate players. Unfortunately, he wasn't invited to the NFL Combine and wouldn't be selected in the 2000 draft. His linebacking partner at UW, Chris Ghidorzi, signed with the Washington Redskins as an undrafted free agent, and Thompson would find a home in Pittsburgh his first season.

He played in eight games his rookie year before the Steelers released him in September 2001. Thompson finished out his playing career in Indianapolis with Peyton Manning as quarterback his final two years.

The Colts struggled to a 6-10 record that 2001 season, which included a five-game losing streak, but former Tampa Bay Buccaneers head coach Tony Dungy was hired to guide the Colts starting in 2002. It was quite the contrasting coaching styles from the previous regime in Indianapolis, as Thompson acknowledged Dungy "was simply the best man I've ever met."

"God first, his family second and football third," exclaimed Thompson, who is currently the Vice President of Sales for Direct Supply out of Milwaukee. "He was one of the best football coaches I've ever been around."

****

After the 1994 season where he recorded 43 tackles and earned UW's Special Teams Player of the Year award, linebacker Chad Cascadden received an opportunity with the New York Jets.

Special teams play helped Chad Cascadden (53) earn All-Rookie team honors with the New York Jets in 1995. | AP Photo

As a walk-on, it was instilled in him to do something in practice to catch the eye of a coach. He believed he could outwork those competing for roster spots. For Cascadden, his objective each day was to get the Jets' coaching staff to notice him in some fashion, whether it was his work ethic or overlooked playmaking ability.

"As an undrafted free agent going into the NFL, I made it a point when I was in practice that I damn near got into a fight every day," Cascadden admitted. "I needed the coach to see that I had passion, that I was not willing to back down, that I was willing to stand up for myself, and that there were very few people on that team that could take me on and win. Ultimately, that led to the opportunity for me to prove myself on the field, which I did, and that's why I had a successful career in the NFL."

That mentality would help him make the 1995 roster for the AFC East organization. He would play in 12 games his first season. Despite a disappointing 3-13 record under head coach Rich Kotite, Cascadden's special teams play earned him all-rookie team honors in 1995 by the Pro Football Writers Association of America.

The Chippewa Falls native played four more years in the league, including the opportunity to be guided by legendary head coach Bill Parcells when Kotite was fired after the 1996 season. During his five seasons, he played in 60 games, starting 12 of them. Statistically, his biggest year was in 1998, where he recorded a career-high five sacks in 13 games.

After his playing days, he stayed in the New York area and now works for the SNY Network as a Jets on-air studio analyst. The special teams extraordinaire carried over the lessons he learned at Wisconsin to the real world.

"Parcells used to say to me, 'Don't show me the pain. Show me the baby. I don't care about how hard it was. Just get it done,'" Cascadden explained. "Whether you're drafted, a walk-on, whether you're oversized or undersized, it doesn't matter. This is about production. That's what I learned the most from Coach Alvarez, Coach Parcells, and Coach

Belichick. At the end of the day, did you get the job done when you were supposed to? That's what people like, right? People love winners."

****

Wisconsin hasn't just produced position players to play on Sundays. Two walk-on long snappers carved out substantial NFL careers of 11 and seven years, respectively. One made a Pro Bowl. The other, well, was actually reluctant to even be a specialist in the first place.

Mike Schneck came to Wisconsin from Whitefish Bay, like his two older brothers before him. One of them, Dan, walked on to the football team and played for Alvarez as a reserve linebacker, earning a letter in 1995. Mike followed in his family footsteps in coming to Madison after being noticed in a camp for specialists by assistant Bernie Wyatt. Schneck wanted to stay at linebacker, but realized he was there to be a long-snapper – a pretty darn good one at that. The coaches took notice of his talents immediately, though Dave Anderson was the incumbent and played that 1995 season.

"Mike had a really good snap," former Wisconsin outside linebackers and special teams coach Jay Hayes said. "About once a day, he'd send one over someone's head, so I started calling him 'One-A-Day,' but you could see he really had talent, so his first year we redshirted him."

The praise from Hayes is significant. He came from California and Notre Dame and had worked with such prominent specialists as punter Craig Hentrich, kicker Ryan Longwell, and long snapper David Binn. Hayes stated "Schnecky" was as good as Binn, who would end up playing as a specialist for 18 years in the NFL with the San Diego Chargers from 1994-2010.

"Mike just had a knack for perfecting his craft and he learned how to get the ball back to the kickers, and make sure the laces were facing the goal post and things like that," said Hayes, who has coached in the NFL since 1999. "We had some really good specialists at that time with Matt

Mike Schneck (54) shares a moment with his son on the Steelers sidelines. | AP Photo

Davenport, Kevin Stempke, Vitaly Pisetsky. We had some really potent weapons and those guys really worked well together."

Schneck solidified the long snapping duties for the Badgers from 1996 through 1998 and that Rose Bowl championship season. He was consistent, though after celebrating Davenport's game-winning field goal against Indiana in September 1997, he dislocated his elbow and would miss a few games. After the 1998 season, he had one year left of eligibility but decided to forego his final year. He didn't necessarily think of going to the NFL at first, as he felt he wasn't good enough.

That would change when Hayes left Wisconsin to become the special teams coach for the Steelers. During the interview process, head coach Bill Cowher noted the team would be looking for a long-snapper. Hayes had just the man.

Schneck stuck and found a home with the legendary NFL franchise for the season, but there was a slight hiccup when initially signing him. With no initial intentions to play professionally, he left without ever formally declaring for the NFL Draft as an underclassman. The league voided the contract after the Steelers initially signed the long snapper, according to Hayes.

"He had to enter the supplemental draft, and there was some consternation there because we were like, 'Oh crap, what if somebody drafts him,' because we weren't going to draft him," Hayes recalled. "He got through it without getting drafted, and we signed him right after. He ended up playing there for quite a while and going to Buffalo and going to Atlanta."

Schneck would play for Cowher for six seasons in Pittsburgh before moving on to the Bills and Falcons for two and three years, respectively. The walk-on mentality kept him working to hone his skill set and paid dividends in the 159 career games he played.

After the 2005 season, he would also receive a distinguished honor and a paid vacation for his efforts. A phone call from one of the Bills' front office personnel delivered the good news: he would make the Pro Bowl, which recognizes and brings out the best players from the league each year to Hawaii.

"I didn't believe them, honestly. I thought they were messing with me," laughed Schneck. "Then you go into a dead panic because you have two weeks to get out there. That's how they did it at the time. We had a little baby, and I hadn't snapped in a month. I was just trying to figure out how to get home and knock the rust off a little bit -- then figure out how to get my family to Hawaii with a little baby. It was totally surreal."

There's always that adage that specialists aren't a "real" part of the team, or are a different breed of football player compared to the rest of the position players. Schneck got to rub elbows with some of the game's best. He wasn't naive to the fact he was there at the Pro Bowl as a long snapper, but all the players he encountered respected him. He even had the opportunity to meet one of the game's all-time greats, though he reciprocated a kind, introductory gesture with a bit of humor.

"I was sitting in my locker, and Peyton Manning actually walked over to me, and said 'Hey, I'm Peyton Manning' I said, 'Yeah I know. I'm Mike Schneck. I think you already forgot who I am.'"

****

Matt Katula played 93 games in his seven seasons between the Ravens, New England Patriots and Minnesota Vikings. Funny thing with the Brookfield native, however, was that he didn't initially want to be a long snapper. In fact, he wanted his talent to be hidden heading into his college recruiting process.

Katula's father played safety and punter in high school, so Matt learned how to long snap at an early age. He played guard and defensive end, but due to the size of the team, he would also be forced to long snap until his senior year. Trying to get some film together to showcase his talents, his mother urged him to add some of those extra skills onto the footage.

"The recruiting process starts, and we're putting together a highlight film," Katula explained. "My mom actually says to me, 'You should put film of the long snapping on this tape.'

"I'm like 'No.' I don't want anyone to know that I can do this. I don't want to get stuck doing it or having to practice it or having anything to do with it."

Katula walked on to Wisconsin after being named first-team all-conference on defense for Waukesha Catholic Memorial, but would find himself behind Jonathan Welsh and future NFL first-round draft pick Erasmus James at defensive end.

Like many freshman, he would have to work through some adjustments in making the jump to Big Ten Football. It

Matt Katula (70) played seven seasons in the NFL. | AP Photo

was a struggle juggling academics with athletic training and preparation for the 2000 Big Ten season.

"I remember my freshman year, I came in and was unblocked on a play," Katula said. "The tight end blocked down. I'm like, 'Oh this is going to be great, I'm going to get a tackle for a loss.' Then (offensive guard Bill) Ferrario hit me so hard I couldn't feel the right side of my body. It was brutal.

"That was kind of my 'Welcome to Division I' moment."

As hard as he worked to display his skills on the defensive side of the ball, his talents at long snapping would lead him to a more pertinent role on the team.

On a Friday walk-through during the 2000 season, Katula was joking around with some teammates and throwing back some snaps. It caught the eye of his head coach. What started as a playful joke with some of his close friends turned into his new calling on the team.

"Alvarez walked up to me and said, 'You're the new backup (long-snapper).'

"I'm like, "Oh my gosh. I can't believe this," Katula laughed. "At the moment, I kind of realized – 'Well wait, I'm a back-up, and (Mike) Solwold's a senior. Oh no, what did I just do?'"

His reaction may not necessarily be one many would feel is appropriate, especially after the godfather of Wisconsin football tells you you're essentially next in line for a prominent position on the team. Depending upon situations and which coverage units you would snap for, a player in his shoes would probably see between five to a dozen snaps per game. He would also have an opportunity to contribute early on as a redshirt freshman. That's something many players in general, let alone a walk-on, would dream of. Yet for the in-state product, he almost felt it wasn't a real position.

"I felt like an outsider and that feeling was real to me," Katula conceded. "That was always tough for me. I wanted to be out there more. I wanted to contribute more, but my skill set didn't lend itself to being out there as an every down player."

Long snappers weren't necessarily a specialized group yet as the modern game's evolved. Most who would "start" at that position were back-ups. Schneck was originally a linebacker, and Mike Solwold before him was a tight end out of Hartland Arrowhead.

Katula would have to come to a realization, that despite fighting the on-going animosity towards the position, he'd have to embrace one of his athletic gifts.

The self-deprecating long-snapper ended up playing in 48 career games for the Badgers in that underrated yet important role on special teams. He put himself in position to be part of some memorable moments including the October 2003 victory against the No. 3 Buckeyes under the lights of Camp Randall Stadium.

Running down an R.J. Morse punt in the third quarter, Katula saw Ohio State cornerback and punt returner Chris Gamble fumble the ball near midfield. He wound up with the recovery, giving Wisconsin possession at the Buckeyes' 38-yard line. The Badgers capitalized with a Mike Allen 38-yard field goal to give Wisconsin a 10-3 advantage as they would go on to upset Jim Tressel and his squad 17-10.

The next morning, Katula stopped at the local McDonalds on Lake Street to grab breakfast. Fresh off the victory, he grabbed a national newspaper. Starting to skim the newspaper, he realized his small play made for some big time coverage.

"I'm looking down, and I see myself on the front page of the *USA Today*. Thought it must be a regional," Katula recalled. "Well, it turns out that it was the national cover, so that is still framed in my basement. I was a little bit heavier then, so I have to explain that when I show people the picture."

Special teams coach Brian Murphy kept pushing Katula to improve upon his skill set, realizing the kid had some potential to make a living as a long-snapper. There was good reason to believe that, as NFL scouts would be at practice and timing his snaps.

After the 2005 Outback Bowl, he signed with Scott Smith and XAM Sports. He didn't head to the NFL Combine, but performed during Wisconsin's pro day that March where he would meet his eventual special teams coach, Gary Zauner.

Katula noted he trusted Zauner, a Milwaukee native, after he ran his pro day. That trust would have an impact in Katula choosing his first professional team he would sign with.

According to the long snapper, he received legitimate

interest from the Dolphins, the Oakland Raiders and Ravens. Miami was actually offering a $5,000 signing bonus, but Smith and Katula couldn't get a Dolphins official back on the phone to confirm. In swooped Zauner and the Ravens, telling Katula he would have a legitimate chance to make the team, but there was a catch: there was no signing bonus.

"So I'm a broke college kid," Katula said. "I have $5,000 sitting there on the table in Miami, and I feel like I'm well positioned to make that team. But then I had the relationship with Gary, and I ended up going to Baltimore for nothing. It worked out my first year there. Like I said, everything happens for a reason."

****

Katula would get the opportunity to play with some of his former Wisconsin teammates in his time with the Ravens. One would be linebacker Nick Griesen, who would suit up in the purple and black for the 2007 and 2008 seasons in wrapping up a seven-year career in the NFL. The second would be his old playmaking safety Jim Leonhard.

Even with his success collegiately – an All-American, all-conference, and school record breaker – his 5-foot-8, 180-pound frame didn't appeal to NFL personnel as a draft pick. Like some of his former teammates had noted, you would never guess he's a professional athlete when passing him on the street. Once again, Leonhard would have to prove them all wrong just as he did at UW.

"Being a free agent, it's the same mentality (as a walk-on)," Leonhard declared. "They have the draft picks that they want to see succeed, and anything they get from a free agent is a bonus. You have to be prepared for that one chance, and if you do well enough in that chance, all of sudden you're going to get one more – and it's doing that over and over and over again until you earn some trust and hopefully make a roster."

Leonhard would sign as an undrafted free agent with the Buffalo Bills in 2005, contributing in 10 games that year.

Like a college freshman trying to pick up a sophisticated defense, Leonhard worked to acclimate quickly to the Bills' schemes. Luckily at Wisconsin, he was exposed to some complicated fronts and coverages.

"Making the jump to the NFL, there are a lot of guys who have played in just one system. They were in one system in high school and college, and all of sudden, they get to the NFL. It's much more complicated and everything seems brand new. Fortunately, I had seen some of the different schemes in college. I had been exposed to that, and it really helped the transition. I was in a very complex 3-4 system, I guess it was kind of 3-4/4-3 – a little bit of both – as a rookie.

"With NFL defenses, you have to be smart and you have to communicate more. That's one of my strengths. It was a blessing to be in that system as a first-year player. It was extremely hard. It is one of those things where you're swimming mentally and not trying to make mistakes, but having some exposure to the schemes in college really did help, because if you can handle it, you stick out. That helped me make the roster and got my foot in the door."

Leonhard played in 38 games in three seasons. In 2007, he started six games in place of injured Ko Simpson, recording 51 tackles and two interceptions in 13 games. Though earning his keep and contributing on both the defense and special teams, the Bills chose not to retain him when free agency came around.

Former Baltimore defensive coordinator Rex Ryan always liked Leonhard coming out of college. The organization had interest in signing the Wisconsin standout for his prowess in the defensive backfield and his punt returning abilities before he chose Buffalo. That interest peaked again once Leonhard was back on the free agent market. Ryan would send him a camp invite in spring 2008, but according to the coordinator, it wasn't a camp invite that would elicit any guarantee of being signed.

"I said, 'Hey let's bring in this Jim Leonhard,' because I always liked him as an athlete," Ryan said. "When we got him in there, after three days, it was pretty obvious the guy

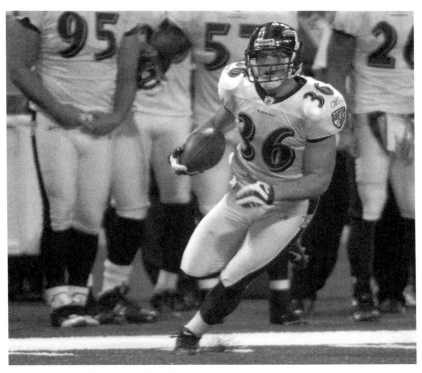

Jim Leonhard (36) helped Baltimore to a number six ranking in total defense in 2007. | AP Photo

was super intelligent, could handle everything we threw at him mentally, and the physical talent -- he just made plays."

The Ravens signed Leonhard on April 29 to compete and earn time behind starters Ed Reed and Dawan Landry. The safety position was stacked for the best defense in the league. Leonhard would fight for a roster spot with draft picks Tom Zbikowski and Haruki Nakamura. Competing with drafted rookies is always difficult because they mostly stick on the roster, but Leonhard showed the same skills and intelligence that made him a Wisconsin legend. By the start of the season, he was the No. 3 safety and also earned a spot as the team's punt returner.

Unfortunately, Landry would suffer a spinal cord concussion in the second game of the year after a collision with Cleveland Browns running back Jamal Lewis. Leonhard, as he's done his entire career to that point, would step in when called upon. Now the quarterback of the defense opposite the playmaker in Reed, the Ravens defense would not skip a beat in that 11-5 season.

In 2007, Baltimore ranked No. 6 in total defense, giving up over 301 yards per game. With Leonhard and such playmakers like Ray Lewis, Bart Scott and Reed, they improved to No. 2 overall, giving up just a shade over 261 yards per game. They allowed just over 15 points per contest jumping up to No. 3 overall in the league. Leonhard more than held his own, registering 69 tackles, one sack and a 35-yard interception return for his only career professional touchdown.

"He's not doing it with a bunch of slackers," Ryan explained in May 2015. "We had the best defense in the league when he came in there. For someone to come in, you better pick it up, and that's what blew us away was how sharp he was. He not only picked it up, he was right up there with Ray, Ed, all of them. Just a sharp guy and knows how to study, knows how to communicate with his teammates. He just did a great job, and I miss him to this day. I wish I had one like him now."

His one-year stay in Baltimore would be a launching point in being viewed as a dependable commodity throughout his 10-year career. He was a combination of athletic ability with the intelligence of a defensive coordinator. The small-town Wisconsin native was on Ryan's wish list when he took over as head coach of the New York Jets in 2009.

Ryan hoped to bring over three Ravens that could replicate the results seen with his previous employer. Each Baltimore expatriate would be for each level of the defense. The Jets targeted Marques Douglas for the defensive line and 2006 second-team All-Pro Bart Scott to guide the linebackers. Leonhard would be contacted immediately after Ryan took over for the Jets.

"I had to have somebody quarterback the defense for me," Ryan said. "He got a call day one. I needed him there, and obviously, I had a vision for him because I knew him. I knew he could quarterback that defense for me and that's exactly what he did."

Thus began the transformation of the Jets defense in 2009, ascending to the No. 1 ranked defense in total yards given up (252.3) and points allowed (14.8). Leonhard contributed 76 tackles to Ryan's defense that season with a career-high 2.5 sacks. Like he did for the Ravens in 2008, he also contributed as a punt returner, averaging 8.2 yards per return in 21 attempts.

His ability to translate the defense helped him become a valuable player-coach on Ryan's teams. Leonhard, an academic All-Big Ten selection from 2002-04, knew it and would play around with the team's assistants.

"He would always claim that he was smarter than Mike Pettine, my defensive coordinator on the Jets," Ryan laughed. "He goes, 'Look, I know this defense better than you do.' He used to kid around with him all the time."

"He took unbelievable notes. He would call the Ravens' defense the 'Old Testament.' Then when we went to the Jets, he called that the 'New Testament.' We were pretty good on defense all those years, and Jim was one of the major reasons."

In Leonhard's final two years with New York, the team would rank third and fifth in the league in total yards given up per game, respectively. Leonhard would also suffer two season-ending injuries in both 2010 and 2011. He rehabbed after knee surgery due to a torn patellar tendon that made him miss the final three games of the 2011 season; this after breaking his right tibia in early December 2010.

The 2010 injury was suffered the Friday before a big Monday night game against the New England Patriots. Without their leader, it would be nearly impossible to diagnose the Patriots' offense like they did in their Week 2, 28-14 win. His absence from the defense was immediately felt, and it showed against Tom Brady a few days later.

"You could hear a pin drop, and we were done. We showed up, but we knew we were done," Ryan conceded. "We

couldn't handle the game plan, and we got absolutely
destroyed 45-3, just absolutely destroyed, humiliated."

"There was no way a back-up could handle that
responsibility. We tried to, but we were leaving guys wide
open all over the place, and it was embarrassing the type of
butt whooping they put on us. That's what I remember
about Jim when he went down – it just devastated
everybody, and for a little guy like he was, he had a huge
impact on our team."

After both injuries, the walk-on wouldn't be retained by
the Jets but would find a home with Manning and the
Denver Broncos for 2012. He ended his career in the same
defensive scheme he mastered. Pettine took over head
coaching duties for the Cleveland Browns after a year in
Buffalo as defensive coordinator. Like Ryan, Pettine brought
his defensive quarterback in Leonhard to the Bills in 2013,
then to the Browns for 2014.

The move to Cleveland would also reunite Leonhard with
another All-American from Wisconsin in Joe Thomas.
Though both weren't as close during their time in Madison
as college standouts, the All-Pro left tackle had a chance to
cement a great friendship with the veteran safety.

"The time that he was in Cleveland was really cool
because we were both older guys on the team," Thomas said,
who is still with the organization. "In the NFL, Wisconsin
guys hang together all the time, so we would spend a lot of
time hanging out together, eating meals, talking. I think we
really grew our bond and our friendship in that time that we
had in the NFL together, and it was amazing."

That player-coach role many saw in Leonhard would be
on full display in transitioning the Cleveland defense to
Pettine's model. Thomas knew those players had a great
leader that would be available for discussions in adjusting to
the new alignments and calls, but Leonhard would also be
thrust into a more prominent role on defense. With an
injury to Taushan Gipson, he wouldn't just be the role
player that instructed his fellow teammates. He would play
in all 16 games, starting the final five.

"Those coaches absolutely loved him in the NFL, for as smart as he was in college football, he was 10 times as smart in the NFL," Thomas declared. "He was the one that had to show every single person on the whole defense where they had to line up. When the Browns brought him in, they expected him to be the back-up safety that would help the young guys, but not play much during the game. Then we ended up having some injuries, and he ended up playing a ton of snaps, and he played really well."

Leonhard's final professional game would come on December 28, 2014 at the stadium where he jump-started his career. The Browns and Ravens would meet in the regular season finale at M&T Stadium in Baltimore. He would also face his former college roommate, and one of his best friends, in Ravens tight end Owen Daniels.

The two had previously faced off in a preseason game when Leonhard briefly spent time with the New Orleans Saints in 2013 before re-signing with Buffalo, while Daniels played his final year in Houston. Their former roommates would refer to the games between Leonhard and Daniels as the "P5 Bowl," a reference to the apartment they shared in the La Ciel complex off-campus in Madison.

On this day Daniels would catch a pass from Ravens quarterback Joe Flacco as Leonhard pushed him out of bounds, but according to Daniels, the play could have been a lot worse.

"It was bad ball security. I didn't have it high and tight," said Daniels of his pass catching form with a laugh. "Jimmy could have gone through me and knocked the ball out of bounds. It was one of those catches where I kind of reached out a bit and didn't have great balance, so I really didn't have any momentum going forward. As I'm making the catch he's coming downhill at me. He could have at the very least got me to the ground if not toss me into the heater that was on the sideline because that was right where we were. I thanked him for a bunch of things after the play. 'Thanks for not throwing me in the heater, thanks for not stripping me, and thanks for not hurting me.'"

The Ravens won 20-10, plummeting the Browns to a 7-9 overall record under Pettine in 2014. Leonhard would finish his final season with 42 tackles and two interceptions, culminating in a career where he recorded 427 tackles, 4.5 sacks and 14 career interceptions. The former All-American returned 108 punts for 9.2 yards per attempt. All of this after not getting a sniff during the 2005 NFL Draft.

For some, it may still amaze a player of his physical stature could amass such a career in the professional game. When you talk to Ryan, Daniels and Thomas, it was never really a question. Leonhard may be the prototypical walk-on in Wisconsin history, but he carved out an impressive NFL career that spanned five teams and a decade of excellence.

"The No. 1 thing I say is you have to be able to play football," said running back Danny Woodhead, a former teammate and close friend of Leonhard's. "You have to have the talent. You have to have the speed. You have to have the agility. You have to have those physical talents. When people said Jimmy was a coach on the field, he was. But this is the thing I always say – he was a great athlete. It wasn't like he was just this guy that 'Oh man, he was so smart and he was at the right spot,' he was a great athlete.

"But there are a lot of guys that have talent. I'm not saying there's a lot of Jimmy Leonhards, but when you're in the NFL, everyone's talented. That's where the mental side comes into play. That's when you need to be a professional, be a pro and learn the schemes, know the playbook and do what it takes to play, even one year. I think that's what it is with Jimmy. Obviously he had talent. Obviously he's smart, and obviously he cared."

****

Chris Maragos grew up cheering for the Green Bay Packers in his hometown of Racine, nearly 150 miles away from "Titletown." During his adolescent years, he fondly remembered watching the return to glory years of the franchise. That culminated in the team's first NFL world championship in nearly three decades on January 26, 1997, as the Packers defeated the New England Patriots 35-21 in Super Bowl XXXI.

Maragos turned 10 years old just 19 days earlier. On that fateful winter evening, he watched his favorite team's players hold up the Lombardi Trophy in New Orleans. How cool it would it be to win an NFL championship? Seventeen years later, his dream became a personal highlight. On February 2, 2014, Maragos and the Seattle Seahawks stunned Manning and the Denver Broncos in a 43-8 route in Super Bowl XLVIII.

The game itself wasn't supposed to be a blowout. On the first offensive play of the game, however, the Broncos set the tone for the rest of the evening as a botched snap by center Manny Ramirez forced running back Knowshon Moreno to fall on the ball in the end zone for a safety. Seattle led 2-0 and would not trail the rest of the game.

Four turnovers doomed the Broncos' chance at its third franchise Super Bowl win. It was former Wisconsin Badgers quarterback Russell Wilson that shined, completing 18-of-25 passes for 206 yards and two touchdown passes for the Seahawks in the lopsided victory.

In a microcosm of his contributions during the 2013 season, Maragos contributed to the team mainly as a special team's ace. He tackled Denver returner Trindon Holliday in the second quarter in a call that was initially ruled a fumble and recovered by Seattle (it was later overturned). He was also one of the leaders of the kickoff return unit that sprung returner Percy Harvin 87 yards for a second half-opening touchdown and a 29-0 lead. The Seahawks were not relenting in their quest for the franchise's first NFL championship.

As he was looking back on his journey during the game, an abundance of memories flooded his thoughts. He admittedly flashed back on his football journey: from a second grader throwing on the shoulder pads for the first time to finding an NFL home in Seattle for three seasons.

"All the stadium steps that I ran, all the hills that I ran, all the workouts, all the tireless hours that I put in watching film, perfecting my craft," Maragos said, "the drills that I did when no one was watching – it almost all just flashed together at one point where it was like it all culminated to this point."

The extra work and effort needed to get noticed paid off. Even though he was underrated, his drive established an edge to fight in the midst of tough circumstances, not just throughout his playing career but in his personal life as well. His devotion to the game and his journey also intersects with his faith, with the latter actually leading him to Madison.

Chris Maragos kisses the Lombardi Trophy following the Seahawks 43-8 victory in Super Bowl XLVIII. | AP Photo

CHAPTER SIX

Faith, Football and Playing for an Audience of One

For Maragos, his journey to the NFL and success in the pro game is one of perseverance through adversity. With no Division I scholarships offered to him, Western Michigan offered the beleaguered prep standout a walk-on chance. He'd be able to redshirt his first season, learning from future NFL standout Greg Jennings.

The opportunity from the Broncos would give Maragos a shot to make an impact in the 2006 season. He broke through the two-deep to be a starter in eight of the 13 games, catching 25 passes that year. His goal of obtaining a scholarship would not be fulfilled, however. There would be a falling out between head coach Bill Cubit and the wide receiver over the scholarship he felt he deserved and, according to Maragos, was discussed between the two parties.

"I always felt as an athlete and my personal conviction was that if I'm going to play my style of play – which is all out, 100 percent everything I have – I have to play for a coach that I 100 percent align with in trust, character, everything," said Maragos. "And so I really felt like some of those things were being compromised by what I was told and what they were doing. I basically said I needed to be somewhere else because I can't play for someone or something that I don't feel 100 percent with, so I decided to transfer."

The souring relationship from the broken commitment led

to Maragos branching out and finding another program. He looked at Division II Grand Valley State, but he set his eyes to a familiar city where he spent a portion of his youth watching football on many Saturdays. He even received some help from Bucky Badger himself.

Well, *a* Bucky Badger.

Chris' brother, Troy, donned the costume of the university's beloved mascot during a portion of his time at the university. A member of Campus Crusades for Christ (CCC, now known as Cru), Troy knew wide receiver Luke Swan through CCC, the parent organization to Athletes in Action, and reached out to him given his younger brother's dilemma. After the introduction, an exchange of Facebook messages then ensued between the two peers.

"He sent his film over during the process," Swan said. "He was really explosive, he was a fast player. He was playing wide out at the time. I saw him, and I thought this dude was a good player. I took the film in, showed it to Coach Mason. He ended up showing it to Coach Bielema."

After a meeting between Maragos and Bielema, another opportunity to walk-on to a Division I program was given to him.

"I just saw a kid on film that was really trying to do everything right," Bielema said. "Seemed like he did a lot of things well. I liked his film so I invited him to walk-on as a wide receiver."

His decision was made up.

"Being from Racine, coming to play at UW was a lifelong dream," Maragos admitted. "I always felt confident in my abilities, and turned down a scholarship offer at Grand Valley State and the opportunity to play right away to have to sit out a year and walk-on at Wisconsin. It was a big risk, but one I was confident in and really felt like the Lord was opening a lot of doors."

"Chris came to Wisconsin," Swan said. "We became roommates, became great friends, and the rest of the story is history."

Faith and football have intersected for many student-athletes, which includes some of Wisconsin's more recognizable walk-ons. Some players' trust in God or relationship with other Christians led them to UW. Some leaned on their faith during struggles on and off the field. They may have all played in front of 80,000 fans at Camp Randall Stadium during their time in Madison, but they played for much more than that – for an Audience of One.

The term Audience of One focuses an individual's performance and one's words, thoughts and actions to be acceptable and pleasing to God rather than the spectators of the world. In athletes' cases, this includes their respective sport. It's a principle that keeps many grounded in their beliefs through the trials and tribulations faced on the field, but also in the game-winning plays and the fame associated with their clutch performances.

It's not uncommon for athletes' social media accounts to show the abbreviation "A01," or a quote of their favorite Bible scripture. Badgers standout running back Melvin Gordon's profile begins with "AO1;" Jared Abbrederis' Twitter profile dedicates himself to his faith: "I am first and foremost a follower of Christ, and use my talents to glorify His name! Strive daily to become a better husband, father, and man of God! #AO1"

Maragos mentions Matthew 6:33 on his Twitter account: "But seek first his kingdom and his righteousness, and all these things will be given to you as well."

His story of faith really bloomed when he was 15, but not under the best of circumstances.

As a teenager, the troubled teen caught himself in a series of events that would ultimately bring him to a crossroads in his early life. The talented football player bought and sold drugs. He was suspended from school for using pepper spray. Maragos admitted he was almost expelled from the school district and was caught vandalizing property around Christmas 2002. He owns up to those mistakes, attributing the character lapse with something many teenagers go through.

"I always like using the analogy that there was this hole

in my heart – this emptiness in that I was trying to fill deep in the world that was going to give me satisfaction," conceded Maragos. "Whether it was being a football player, whether it was getting people to like me, whether it was buying stuff, having stuff, using drugs, whatever it might be, I fell into a lot of those pitfalls trying to find my satisfaction."

He committed himself to his faith, and the tide turned around. After transferring to Racine Horlick his senior season, FCS program Illinois State offered a scholarship, but he drew late interest from the coaching staff at Western Michigan and decided to walk on to the MAC program.

The coaching staff still kept him at wide receiver when he arrived in Madison, but would have to sit out the 2007 season. The Racine product had to prove the naysayers wrong yet again, who questioned his leap of faith instead of heading to Grand Valley State.

A new position would be calling in the spring

Chris Maragos (21) goes up high to intercept a pass intended for Michigan State wide receiver Mark Dell (2). | AP Photo

of 2008. According to Swan, Maragos ran a comeback route and the quarterback was late with the ball. A defender got in front of him and intercepted it, sprinting towards the end zone. Not one to take a play off, Maragos took off after in pursuit. What happened next would shape the Wisconsin secondary for the next two seasons and for Maragos' career.

"Normally, what you do when someone gets an interception is that you go tag off on him," Swan said. "Chris was 10 yards behind – he took off running like a shot. He closed the gap and right about the 10-yard line, he leapt and tackled the player and knocked the ball out."

"I don't know what possessed me to do it, but I was always in competition mode," Maragos said, recalling his effort with a hint of remorse. "Whether it was in practice or drills or whatever, I was always in game mode. Looking back, I kind of felt bad because I thought they'd kick me off the team since you're not supposed to do that."

Quite the contrary, actually.

"What I saw instinctively, I thought he read things very well, so I asked him to play safety," Bielema recalled. "He thought I was crazy."

Maragos trusted his head coach's decision, however, despite not playing defense since high school. The results paid off early.

In the 2008 spring game, he picked off an Allan Evridge pass in his first simulated game time action in the defensive backfield. The season itself wouldn't be Wisconsin's or Bielema's greatest year. UW managed a 7-6 record that season that ended with a disappointing 42-13 loss to Florida State in the Champs Sports Bowl. However, Maragos worked his way into Wisconsin's secondary rotation. Playing in all 13 games, he would replace incumbent Shane Carter and start in six. He finished seventh on the team in tackles with 45 and recorded his first career interception against Illinois on October 25.

Another season meant another year to sharpen his tools spiritually and on the field, but two honors were bestowed upon him prior to the 2009 campaign.

First, Maragos and Watt would be notified in the spring that they would both be placed on scholarship. Feelings of validation and respect flowed through Maragos after earning the respect of the coaching staff and being awarded the free ride, but there was one more accolade to come. Heading into that season, his Wisconsin teammates voted him as one of the team captains, a distinction Maragos still holds dear to his heart.

"For me, and I can say this wholeheartedly, that is by far the single greatest accomplishment in my football career up to this point," Maragos proclaimed.

"It hasn't been winning a Super Bowl. It hasn't been getting put on scholarship. It wasn't getting nominations and voting for a Pro Bowl. None of that. Being named a team captain is my greatest accomplishment because it represented something so much more than an athletic achievement. Your own teammates, the guys you sweat with, bleed with, sacrifice with, for them to promote you to be a captain is the greatest accomplishment I've ever had. Because when you earn the respect of those around you there's no greater compliment in life."

Maragos grew more comfortable in the secondary in his redshirt senior year, starting all 13 games and leading the team with four interceptions. One came in the second overtime of a 34-31 thriller between UW and Fresno State on September 12. That interception and a fourth-down pass breakup contributed to two early wins during that 2009 season. The team finished 10-3, with a solid 20-14 win over No. 14 Miami in the 2009 Champs Sports Bowl that would springboard the program to three consecutive Rose Bowl trips.

After the season, he turned his attention to the professional game and his prospects in the NFL; like his mentor in Leonhard, he went undrafted. He played football most of his life, but was still two years into learning the nuances of the safety position. Maragos signed with the San Francisco 49ers and survived most of the 2010 training camp until being cut on September 3. It would be a roller coaster of transactions thereafter: he would be signed to the practice squad, then promoted to the active roster; then released, re-signed to the practice squad, then activated again before the season would end.

He leaned on his wife, Serah, who he met at Western Michigan, as well as his faith to endure through the bleak periods early in his professional football career where he didn't see the bigger picture unfolding.

"For me, having to bide my time, it was hard," Maragos admitted. "It was difficult. I didn't understand why. I thought I was good enough to play. I didn't know why it was happening, but I knew I just had to stay faithful. I knew I had to stay obedient and just continue to work hard and just maximize everything I had in my opportunities."

That big picture began to unfold to the benefit of his career. After being cut by the 49ers in September 2011, the Seahawks picked him up onto their practice squad then activated him a month after signing him. He became part of the vaunted Legion of Boom, ultimately won a world championship, and developed into one of the NFL's key special teams standouts.

After moving to Philadelphia after the 2013 season, he helped the Eagles become one of the NFL's top-ranked special teams units. That year, he paced the team with 14 special teams tackles while forcing a fumble and partially-blocking a punt. He showed a knack at creating points, as he scored his first professional touchdown after a blocked punt against the St. Louis Rams. For his efforts in that inaugural season with Philadelphia, he was voted as a second alternate for the Pro Bowl. Maragos would continue creating havoc on special teams in 2015 with a blocked punt against the New England Patriots in a stunning 35-28 upset victory.

The former walk-on has worked his way up to making football a living. From his adolescence to his current profession on Sundays, he is an underdog that proved his worth despite setbacks on a road less traveled. His faith and his work ethic drove him to the success he's seeing on the field heading into the 2016 season.

"Whether you're at the top of your game, (or)the bottom," Maragos said, "whether you're a Super Bowl champion or not, having an established fighter mentality in you to always want to get better, always want to be great, always take care of the details, never cut corners, it's really helped mold and shape a lot of what I've been able to do in my NFL career."

****

Luke Swan was a two-time, all-state selection by the Wisconsin Football Coaches Association (WFCA), catching 121 passes for 2,234 yards and 26 touchdowns in his prep career. He was only rated a two-star recruit by Scout, one-star by Rivals, but camped at Wisconsin in his prep years to get on the Badgers' radar. He was offered and later accepted a walk-on opportunity.

He was a big fish in a small pond back in Fennimore, a town of approximately 2,500 residents in southwestern Wisconsin, but he had to adjust to Division I football. The transition to the college game was initially a tough road. There were moments when the receiver wondered if the process was worth it, especially with being buried at the bottom of the depth chart behind some of the best receivers to come through Wisconsin in Lee Evans, Brandon Williams, and Jonathan Orr.

He pushed through it due to a foundation rooted in faith and a work ethic instilled in his upbringing by his parents, Scott and Chris. He also found solace in speaking with Athletes in Action campus director Scott Mottice, who became a mentor. He'd join the group to interweave his faith and sport.

"I would say him, along with some other student-athletes, that are like-minded in their faith," Swan said, "it really started to grow and mature in me and really get me to a place where I realized this is where God wanted me, and this is where an opportunity was to serve Him."

Swan only played in one game his redshirt freshman year and saw the field in eight games in 2005, though he did not

Luke Swan (1) makes one of his many clutch catches versus the University of Buffalo. | AP Photo

catch a pass. He had a position coach in Henry Mason that would stay on him to ensure his technique and route running were right so when the time came he could be successful.

The walk-on admitted some days Mason was rough on him, but Swan realized he needed to perfect his craft further to contribute in a greater fashion to Paul Chryst's pro-style offense.

Mason believed Swan was on the precipice of breaking out, but injuries hindered him from making an impact. He credited his receiver with not giving up when adversity hit and also how he wasn't afraid of doing the dirty work of a receiver in Wisconsin's offensive scheme. That meant being blocking effectively for backs like Brian Calhoun and P.J. Hill.

The star started to shine brightly for Swan during spring practices in 2006. A new frame of mind emerged that rejuvenated his confidence heading into his fourth season as a redshirt junior. He earned a spot as one of the back-up wide receivers on the depth chart after spring ball behind Marcus Randle-El. Greater things would be on the horizon for the walk-on, however.

"We went through spring ball, we thought he had an opportunity to start," Mason said. "I brought him in a week before training camp in August and I told him the spot is yours to lose. You're going to go into camp, and you're going to be a first-team guy so you need to take the ball and run with it."

The pressure to perform would be heightened even further after Randle-El tore his ACL during fall camp, which would keep him out the rest of the year. All the hammering, drilling, yelling and corrections in the film room would pay off for Swan with an explosive year on the field. One more change, a material one, would be made prior to the season starting that would further fuse faith and football in Swan's life.

The No. 1 jersey was worn previous seasons by Williams and Ahmad Merritt before that, as it was designated as a wide receiver's number for years. Mason, who coached receivers from 1995-2007, approached Swan and asked if he would wear it.

"I wasn't a big fan of guys wearing that jersey, but the thing about it is, if you're going to wear that jersey, then you need to be *that guy*," stated Mason, who is currently Wisconsin's director of player personnel and external relations. "With Luke, if you threw it out there, he took it as a challenge. He took it and ran with it. He was one of the more productive No. 1s in the program."

There was hesitancy on Swan's part, especially with filling the number previously worn by the school's all-time receptions leader. But a trip to the Ultimate Training Camp in Fort Collins, Colo., that summer before the season – a camp put on by Athletes in Action – made him recalibrate his initial feelings.

"At first, I kind of said, 'Nah, I don't know if I want to change numbers," Swan acknowledged. "I'd been No. 15, but then I thought about it for a second. I was like 'Man, what an awesome thing for me to be reminded every single day I go to practice that I'm wearing No. 1 representative of the Audience of One concept.'"

Swan accepted the offer from Mason with the hope his jersey change would facilitate dialogue with fans and teammates about his spirituality off the field. On the field, he worked in tandem with fellow walk-on Paul Hubbard, playing in all 13 games that season, including 10 starts. He caught 35 receptions for 595 yards, but led the team in yards per catch and tied for the team lead with five touchdowns.

He earned team offensive player of the week honors after a four-catch, 85-yard performance in a come from behind victory against Illinois. His 42-yard, go-ahead touchdown capped his first career 100-yard receiving game in a 24-21 win at Iowa on November 11. His contributions led to a school record 12 wins that season, capping it off with a 17-14 win over No. 12 Arkansas in the Capital One Bowl.

Patience and perseverance paid off.

2007 was shaping up to be a huge season, as Swan was named as one of the five team captains with fellow former walk-ons Ken DeBauche and Ben Strickland. Swan's year started off red hot, as he reeled in 21 catches through five games for the Badgers.

Heading into an October 6 date with Illinois in Champaign, UW was undefeated and Swan led all the wide receivers in receptions, but another obstacle was about to be thrown in his way that would test his faith.

Down by 17 points early UW clawed its way back to make it a two-score game on multiple occasions. Swan had already snagged four catches for 67 yards on the afternoon, but his season would change drastically when he landed in an awkward manner making a catch late in the second quarter during UW's comeback attempt.

"We kind of drew it up on the sidelines. It was something we hadn't practiced," Swan recalled about the play where he was injured. "I remember talking with (quarterback) Tyler Donovan on the sidelines. We thought we could get something big in that area. I probably ran it a little bit too deep, and Tyler was a little bit late because we didn't have the timing right. So when I caught the ball and landed awkwardly, it was like I was a hurdler going over a hurdle.

"Then the safety just had a little bit more time to come up and lay a hit, so it was just one of those in the wrong position, wrong place, and your leg caught straight outside and you're hit from behind."

Swan recalled he wasn't in much pain, but the injury was devastating. He didn't realize until later that trainers were dragging his leg behind him as they took him off the field. Tests revealed he tore his hamstring completely off the bone. Through the bleak outlook and the devastating injury, Swan appeared unchanged on the outside.

"He carried the same demeanor like he had prior to the injury, and I'm just staring at this cat like, 'How does he maintain that kind of composure at such a young age?'" former UW defensive back Aaron Henry said, now a Rutgers assistant coach. "To have the type of season he was having, and then all of sudden, not really lose it, but lose the ability to play the game at the level that he wanted to play at?"

Pastor Matt Metzger, who traveled to the hospital to be with and pray for Luke for the impending surgery, was impressed with how he was handling the situation. Then again, Metzger saw Swan from the start of his collegiate career. That grounded faith and attitude never changed regardless if he was buried on the depth chart, the No. 1 receiver, or facing the long, six-month road ahead to recovery.

"He continued to be this young guy who was just willing to say, 'I'm going to trust God in the midst of all of this, and I'm not going to look to the circumstances or to what my hopes and dreams were of whatever this was going to turn out to be. I'm trusting in God and in Him alone for this entire situation because God has better dreams for my life than I do,'" remembered Metzger, who currently is the Lead Pastor for Blackhawk Church's downtown location in Madison.

"It just blew me away. It really did."

That's not to say there wasn't internal frustration brewing in Swan. With his NFL dream dashed, an identity struggle ensued without playing football.

"Through trial, I've learned that's the time you grow the most, and I grew as a man in learning how to deal with something where your hopes are in something," Swan said. "It also solidified who I was and where my identity is. I had to really not only say it but profess it with the way that I handled myself and internally just processed it."

"Luke's been a guy who I've looked up to, just for the way he's carried and conducted himself as a Christian, as a football player, as a man, as a husband, as a father. I mean the guy is as good as it gets," Maragos declared about his teammate and close friend. "I've always tried to emulate a lot of the things that he's done. We were able to hold each other accountable and keep each other on the straight and narrow, so that was awesome to have."

That last play at Memorial Stadium would end up being the last regular season game action Swan took part in, despite briefly signing with the Kansas City Chiefs in 2008, and participating in Michael Irvin's television reality show, "4th and Long," for a roster spot with the Dallas Cowboys. His professional football dreams may have been cut short, but surprisingly, Swan called it the "best thing that's happened to him." Without the injury and the journey it led him on, he wouldn't have met his wife and set him on his current path.

"I needed to go through that to gain the maturity that I needed to move on in life and become the man that I needed to be, to raise a family, to be a husband, all of those things."

****

Another opportunity with football opened up for Swan

down the road as he returned to Wisconsin from 2011 to 2014 as an offensive graduate assistant. What makes his time at UW even more special, like his former teammate in Strickland, is the fact he played or coached under three of the four head coaches in the modern Wisconsin era. The former wide receiver played under Alvarez and Bielema, then coached under Bielema and Gary Andersen. He saw how all three coached the team, along with their styles in developing and handling walk-ons at Wisconsin.

Swan worked with Jared Abbrederis, another walk-on who would end up leaving a huge imprint on Badgers football. They were similar. Both were from small towns: Abbrederis from Wautoma, Wis. Swan from Fennimore. Both were multi-sport studs in high school. Swan lettered in four sports, while Abbrederis led Wautoma/Faith Christian to the Division II state title in track and field in 2009. Their deep faith also showed a grounded attitude that helped propel them to their legacy as Wisconsin wide receivers despite struggles and successes.

"We really got to know each other on a deep level that way," Swan said. "We had some really good conversations. His wife got to know my wife. A lot of those things were cool, to be part of his journey and pass on some of the things that I experienced, and to push him the few years that we were together when I was a 'GA' and he was a player."

There were some differences between the two, however.

"I would say, first of all, he's much more accomplished and he's done more than me," Swan laughed. "He's one-upped me, which the competitor in me is like, 'Man, I wish I could have done a little bit more,' but at the same time super excited for him."

When comparing their games, Swan admitted Abbrederis was faster and more of a deep ball threat in open space than he was as the "Z" (field) receiver during most of Swan's coaching days in Madison. Swan focused more on the route tree and working within "tight spaces" in being a boundary, or "X" receiver, as a player.

Unlike his predecessor, Abbrederis had to convert to wide

receiver during his transition to college. He was an option quarterback who led the Hornets to a WIAA Division IV state crown in football in 2008, but in a pro-style system, his option skills would not be required.

Abbrederis also came to Wisconsin looking to perform both on the track and football teams, similar to a long line of former Badgers including Joe Thomas, Paul Hubbard, Kyle Jefferson, and Michael Bennett. He was recruited to be a decathlete by men's track and field coach Ed Nuttycombe, and there were some high hopes for his future in that sport.

Jared Abbrederis (4) breaks away from a Penn State defender for a big gain. | AP Photo

"I know the track coaches here desperately wanted Abbrederis," UWBadgers.com's Andy Baggot said, who's covered Wisconsin-based sports for 38 years. "They saw an Olympic-caliber decathlete in Abbrederis, and he was incredibly gifted. They had some thought, if not an Olympic-caliber then an NCAA-champion decathlete."

Like most first-year college players, the transition to a

full-time football schedule was daunting and exhausting. Abbrederis would only see action on the scout team for football, including some time back at quarterback during the 2009 season to prepare for opponents who had running quarterbacks.

It was a struggle the first semester on campus, and in the interest of not just "being a guy" in two athletic programs, he was weighing his options and leaning towards concentrating on track. There was a nudge from backup quarterback Jon Budmayr, who worked out and threw the ball with Abbrederis during the offseason.

"He was an unbelievable track runner and kind of saw some opportunities there that were more immediate than football, and so that caught his eye early on. It wasn't so much talks that we had, although we definitely had conversations about it," said Budmayr, who noted both would stand up in each other's weddings.

"When you first get up to the university, you're kind of searching. You don't know anybody. You're kind of hoping to hit it off with someone that has the same interests and same drive as you. Abby was always willing. If I asked 10 guys to catch and nine of them said they couldn't make it, Abby would be the one that was there. That showed me right away that he was willing to work for whatever he was going to get. As he was working through that with football and track and going back and forth, that kind of sparked whatever that was inside of him that kind of got him interested in football. There was nothing special I did. It was just 'Hey I'm trying to throw here and trying to get better, and you know what, you're not that bad of a receiver either.' I think he found that out as he worked through it and gained his confidence as he got more reps."

With injuries to some wide receivers in spring 2010, Abbrederis was able to climb the depth chart and showcase his abilities against starting cornerbacks Antonio Fenelus and Niles Brinkley. He stuck with football as his sport from then on, but also rededicated himself to his faith.

"My first semester was tough for me," Abbrederis

admitted, "but after that I finally just gave over my life and really got back to Bible studies and just plugging myself in and getting myself involved."

One of those bible studies would not just provide accountability and a deepening of his faith. He would also find the love of his life, as he met his future wife, Rachel, through a life group led by Metzger and his wife later in 2010.

His interest in the church and ministry peaked to the point of interning at Blackhawk before his senior season. In that time, he worked with the high school ministry department in between team workouts during that summer, which gave him a chance to development relationships with teenagers about their faith and challenges they face.

"I think the thing that he appreciated was that he was able to come onto our staff at Blackhawk and just be Jared – not Jared the football player, not Jared who had done amazing things, not Jared who might head to the Packers – but just Jared," Metzger said.

By the 2010 season opener against UNLV, he found himself in the two-deep of the wide receiver corps behind Nick Toon. He contributed during that first of three consecutive Rose Bowl years, hauling in 20 receptions for 289 yards and three touchdowns. His first collegiate touchdown was a three-yard strike from quarterback Scott Tolzien in the first quarter of a 41-23 win over Minnesota.

Following Wisconsin's 11-2 co-Big Ten Championship and Rose Bowl berth, Abbrederis' role in the offense was set to expand even further with David Gilreath, Isaac Anderson and Jefferson all exhausting their eligibility. Like Maragos and Swan before him, Abbrederis also attended the Ultimate Training Camp before that redshirt sophomore season, further focusing in on his faith that would positively translate on to the field.

His ascension through the depth chart warranted a scholarship opportunity. Both he and Ethan Hemer worked their way into the first or second teams ("the two-deep") of UW's depth-chart. It appeared they were in line to become the next walk-ons to receive scholarships, but a game-changing transfer quarterback by the name of Russell Wilson would change that. Bielema needed to give a scholarship to one of the newest Badgers, but that would leave out one or the other two former walk-ons. Neither received the lone scholarship left for the fall semester heading into the 2011 season.

"Obviously, 'Abby' went on to become a very, very good player, but we had to give him a scholarship one semester later than I had hoped, but it wasn't against anything that I had promised," Bielema recalled, noting he didn't want to split a scholarship between the two deserving members of his team.

It was a tough pill to swallow not just for Abbrederis, but for his family.

"I mean, my parents don't have a lot of money – my dad's a firefighter and my mom's a stay-at-home-mom – and they really couldn't help out as much," Abbrederis said. "I just had to call my grandparents and try to get some money just to get through that semester, because then after that semester Coach Bielema said he would put us on scholarship.

"It was tough, but with a player like Russell throwing you the ball, it kind of helps out, too."

Despite the disappointment of not going on scholarship until 2012, Abbrederis provided a perfect complement to Toon in a high-powered offense that scored 44.1 points per game. He finished the year with 55 receptions for a team-leading 933 yards with eight touchdowns. As a punt returner, he finished third in the nation ahead of future NFLers Tyrann Mathieu and Tavon Austin. His 346 total yards in the 2012 Rose Bowl loss against the Oregon Ducks, were the most ever gained by a Wisconsin player in a bowl game.

With Toon leaving after 2011, Abbrederis would be UW's lone, true receiving threat in his final two seasons. Both years he finished as a first-team All-Big Ten selection, and led the team in receptions and receiving yards. He'd even complete a pass to quarterback Curt Phillips for 27 yards in the 2013 Big Ten Championship game against Nebraska where the Badgers shell-shocked the Huskers 70-31.

His senior campaign netted him 78 receptions, a single season school record, for 1,081 yards and eight touchdowns. That included lighting up future first-round draft pick Brandon Roby and an Ohio State secondary to the tune of 10 receptions for 207 yards and a touchdown in a 31-24 loss at the Horseshoe. He finished his career tied as Wisconsin's all-time receptions leader with 202 and tied for second in career touchdown receptions (23). For his efforts in 2013, he also took home the Burlsworth Trophy, given to the nation's most outstanding player that began his career as a walk-on.

"I wouldn't change being a walk-on for anything," Abbrederis declared. "Just the type of mentality you have coming out of this. You learn a lot going through it about how hard work and dedication can overcome people overlooking you, and to earn that, not everybody can do that."

Abbrederis trained in California then competed in the Senior Bowl and at the NFL Scouting Combine. Mock drafts had him selected between the second and sixth rounds. The first and second days came and went without his name being called at the podium. Finally, the call came on the 176th overall pick of the draft, in the fifth round, by his hometown Green Bay Packers.

"It was pretty stressful," Abbrederis recalled on draft day, "but when you finally get the call, it was pretty special just being around all the family and then obviously your phone is blowing up after that. It was definitely the team I wanted to be on."

Abbrederis didn't have to travel far to make the 90-mile trip up to Green Bay from his hometown in Wautoma, but it would be over a year's time before he played in a game on the hallowed grass of Lambeau Field. He went through the rookie minicamp, then organized team activities and June camp sessions, but his right knee became sore during the first week of training camp. He even kept practicing a day after the initial soreness to work through the pain, but something was off.

Tests confirmed a torn ACL, and his rookie season would be lost to rehabbing and re-strengthening his knee.

Abbrederis stayed in Green Bay and continued to train for the 2015 season, and he would have to compete with a logjam of talented receivers on the Packers' roster like

Abbrederis will look to make a bigger impact with the Packers in 2016. | AP Photo

All-Pros Jordy Nelson and Randall Cobb, second-year receiver Davante Adams, Jeff Janis and Myles White. Then came Ty Montgomery, a 2015 third-round draft pick who many thought would slide into the depth chart as the natural No. 4 receiver.

Gaining mental reps and following practice and each play was one thing while on the sidelines in 2014, but cementing the play assignments, the calls, the individual signals assigned by quarterback Aaron Rodgers into his memory would have to be done on the field. All signs pointed to a return to start training camp to battle for a roster spot, but he would have to wait. Again.

That first day of training camp in late July, Abbrederis suffered a concussion that would keep him out for over a month until he was cleared to return on the last Tuesday of practices. That was two days before the Packers would play their final preseason game against the New Orleans Saints at Lambeau Field. At last, he would be able to play extensively for the first time since the Badgers' loss in the Capital One Bowl on Jan. 1, 2014 – a span of close to twenty months.

Only receiving a game's worth of snaps, Abbrederis showed a flash with his punt returning skills in averaging over 11 yards per return. Even with a decent game's showing, he admitted that he expected to be cut due to the lack of film on him. Though an ACL tear to Nelson and lingering injuries would be a concern to the receiving corps, he was amongst the last released to trim the roster down to 53 players.

His faith, like Swan's, kept him grounded through another challenging time.

"I'm not really worried about all that," Abbrederis said when referring to his thought process and NFL prospects after being cut. "Whatever happens, happens. God has a plan. Whether it was playing football or doing something else, I wasn't really worried about it."

No one claimed him off of waivers, and Green Bay signed him to their practice squad on September 7. It took a few weeks to get back into game-ready shape, as he was admittedly tired in his only preseason action. The conditioning kicked in at the right time, however, as injuries to the wide receiving corp continued to decimate one of the league's deeper groups. Adams suffered an ankle sprain against the Seattle Seahawks on September 20, and after a month on the practice squad – Abbrederis was signed to the active roster on October 3.

His first catch of his professional career came on a 15-yard reception on a 3rd-and-1 pass from Rodgers during an 18-16 loss to the Detroit Lions. He finished the game with four catches for 57 yards, including a 32-yard catch on a drive that helped bring the Packers back within two points in the third quarter. Unfortunately on that play, he suffered a rib injury that would keep him out until the second match-up against the Lions on December 3. Another setback, but a relatively minor one, all things considered.

Playing time increased with his knowledge of and confidence in the offense, along with more injuries to the receivers, as Montgomery would miss the bulk of the season due to a high ankle sprain. Abbrederis, who primarily worked in the slot in four wide receiver sets until that point, would see even more action in the playoffs.

When Adams suffered a knee injury against the Washington Redskins in the NFC Wild Card game, the former walk-on jumped in and caught two passes for 14 yards. He also scored on a two-point conversion – a checkdown to him in the slot on the right side of the field. That reception extended the lead to a 14-point advantage in what would be Green Bay's 35-18 victory.

The Wisconsin native caught four more passes in a crazy 26-20 overtime loss at Arizona. His six receptions in the playoffs complemented his nine catches for 111 yards during the regular season. He provided a knack for moving the chains, as five of those nine were for first downs.

Despite a resurgent showing towards the end of the year, Abbrederis had his work cut out for him heading into the 2016 season. Returning are a healthy Nelson and Montgomery, along with Cobb, Adams, Janis and others that are primed to compete for significant playing time. General manager Ted Thompson also selected speedy California wide receiver Trevor Davis in the fifth round of the draft.

His hard work and talent translated positively to the field during OTAs and training camp in 2016. Going up against a loaded wide receivers group, Abbrederis earned a roster spot and a spot in the Packers' offense.

Despite any external pressures that may present themselves, he had reassurance in whatever happens on the field and in the locker room.

"I never really worried about it, obviously you have all your goals and aspirations, but whatever God's plan is for you, that's what's going to happen," he avowed calmly. "You set your goals and you try to work as hard as possible to achieve them, but if you do everything you can and it doesn't work out, you can rest easy in your preparation and all the hard work you put in and knowing that God has a plan."

****

Abbrederis had the opportunity to hear his name announced on draft weekend, to get that phone call from an NFL team who would allow him a shot to live out his dream. His former teammate, fullback Bradie Ewing, would also be fortunate enough to hear his name in the fifth round in 2012.

Prior to his time in the NFL and at UW, the *Wisconsin State Journal* awarded Ewing their All-Area Player of the Year honors in 2007 after gaining 2,116 yards and 24 touchdowns his senior year. He was also named first-team all-state by the WFCA, second-team all-state by the Associated Press as a running back.

Initially focused on the basketball court in high school, he realized football would be the best avenue to play at the next level. UW's football staff presented an opportunity as a preferred walk-on, a deal that Bielema confirmed would be a "two and three" type deal. Ewing would pay the first two years of college, then start on scholarship his third academic year. FCS program North Dakota offered a scholarship but as a linebacker rather than running back. For Ewing, like many other in-state kids, UW's offer was too good to pass up.

Ewing impressed the coaching staff early on, and his performance during 2008's fall camp earned significant time on the kickoff and kickoff return units his freshman year. He even scored his first collegiate touchdown during Wisconsin's 51-14 throttling of Marshall. He finished the year with four special teams tackles and earned his first letter.

After that freshman year, the position change to fullback started. He mostly worked on special teams again while battling through shoulder and groin injuries in the spring and summer camps in 2009, but a transformation evolved over the four years he played in Madison, converting into a bruising, punishing fullback. The athletic back learned to lower his center of balance while finishing his blocks. Ewing added 30 pounds to keep up as a Big Ten fullback, and he acclimated to playing at that weight.

"It was pretty tough," Ewing admitted. "It was easy for me as a running back to run physical, but it took me a while to transition to blocking as a fullback."

Heading into the 2010 season, redshirt freshman Ryan Groy, an offensive lineman, would wear No. 47 and even started the season opener at fullback at UNLV. While the nimble, 300-pound Middleton native was used in some "heavy" packages that would require bigger personnel to move the chains, Ewing was versatile enough to be a threat in the passing game while clearing the way for the tailbacks behind him. Many know Ewing as one of the most genuine and friendly people they've met off the field, but he developed a punishing demeanor to the role he thrived in his final two years.

"I feel like that's something I always tried to do a good job at," Ewing stated. "When you step between the lines, you're playing ball. It may require you to be nasty, especially as a fullback when you're lead blocking."

He gradually took on more of a definitive role in the offense as the season progressed. Ewing wouldn't technically get his first start at fullback until the fifth game of the season at Michigan State.

One of the most productive games of the year, and the one where everything really clicked for him at fullback, came in their 31-30 win at No. 13 Iowa on October 23. Starting his second game, he got in on the scoring action quickly, catching a seven-yard touchdown off a perfectly executed play-action fake. Wisconsin would sport a 10-6 lead in the second quarter.

He opened holes for John Clay and Montee Ball, acting as the lead blocking back for their three combined rushing

Bradie Ewing (34) served as a Badger captain in the 2011 season. | AP Photo

touchdowns. That included Ball's eight-yard, game-winning score. Ewing also continued his contributions on special teams. A week prior, he provided a key block on David Gilreath's 97-yard kickoff return for a touchdown in UW's 31-18 upset over No. 1 Ohio State. Against the Hawkeyes, Ewing blocked for punter Brad Nortman on his 17-yard run in the fourth quarter. The play call, known as "Chains," extended their drive that led to Ball's score.

"It was just an awesome game," Ewing bluntly stated. "So many guys laid out all game."

The former two-star recruit followed up that junior season with a more prominent role in 2011, earning a captain title alongside Wilson, Patrick Butrym, and Henry. Starting eight games, the human battering ram opened up holes for Ball, the Heisman Trophy finalist, who gained 1,923 yards and scored 33 rushing touchdowns. He became a potent option in the passing game, catching 20 passes for 246 yards from

Wilson, and was the Special Teams Player of the Year.

The hard work through four years at Wisconsin, combined with training at NX Level, paid off. He joined another former Badgers standout in offensive lineman Peter Konz in Atlanta, who was selected in the second round.

The next three seasons, however, Ewing battled season-ending injuries at the professional level. While competing for the starting fullback spot, his knee "gave out and popped" when trying to block a defender on special teams in the first preseason game of the 2012 season. He was diagnosed with a torn ACL and his rookie year would be cut short before it began.

After a sports hernia operation in the offseason, he progressed and made the 2013 Falcons' roster. He started the first two games, hauling in two receptions for 29 yards, but his year would end there. During that 31-24 win over the St. Louis Rams, Ewing tore and separated his shoulder. Atlanta head coach Mike Smith announced the star-crossed fullback would be put on season-ending IR for the second time in two years. Frustration after another significant setback was apparent, but he leaned on his faith.

"I truly believe that was because God has a master plan and that through that adversity, I got to spend more time at home with my wife early in our marriage, and that was awesome," Ewing declared. "I was able to connect with a lot of people throughout the community in Atlanta through all that adversity."

Struck down twice, Ewing would push one last time to continue playing in the NFL. Back to NX Level, back to the grind of proving he could compete and earn a spot on a team's roster, but not with the Falcons. On March 21, 2014, Atlanta released the fullback, placing him on waivers. He wouldn't be without a team for very long.

The Jacksonville Jaguars, with new general manager Dave Caldwell, claimed him four days later. Caldwell was Atlanta's former director of personnel in charge of college and pro scouting efforts when Ewing was drafted. He had been hired to rebuild the AFC South franchise with new head coach Gus Bradley. Ewing would get that fresh start five hours south of Atlanta but, a third IR trip would effectively end the comeback. In the second preseason game, Ewing was blocking a Chicago Bears defender when he tore a ligament in his wrist.

Third season. Third season-ending injured reserve designation. Throughout that time, Ewing prayed for guidance whether it was worth continuing to play football or move on. In early spring of 2015, the Jaguars formally released him.

"Just continually, I felt like I was getting shown a different path – with the injuries, through the adversity I faced, it just continued to mold me into the person I am," Ewing said. "Football gave me some awesome experiences, awesome relationships, but I kind of just felt like it was maybe time, and He was showing me it was time to turn that page."

The Wisconsin product wouldn't have to look very far for the next chapter of his life, however. His former offensive coordinator, Chryst, was back at UW as head coach. Ewing would find a home as one of the Badgers' assistant strength and conditioning coaches. He came back to Madison to work for his alma mater, where he played in 52 games in his collegiate career, where he started in his final two seasons, and where he was named captain by his peers for the 2011 season.

CHAPTER SEVEN

Breaking Through

From day one, Ewing contributed on the field at Wisconsin. He played in 52 games during his UW career, an impressive feat for any college football player, let alone a walk-on. Eight players, including walk-ons Drew Meyer and Ethan Hemer, hold the school record with 54.

Walk-ons like Hemer, Ethan Armstrong, and Ewing heavily contributed to the success of the teams they played on, whether starting for a single season or for several.

Hemer turned down opportunities at Miami (Ohio), Eastern Michigan, and Illinois State to come to UW. In the same recruiting class as Armstrong, Jared Abbrederis, and Kyle Zuleger, the raw, small-town prospect broke through the depth chart his redshirt freshman year and made a significant impact on Wisconsin's defensive fronts.

"He's probably the most improved player from day one to Senior Day of anybody in our class," teammate Chris Borland proclaimed.

Hemer made his mark early on, and though he officially redshirted in 2009, players and coaches took notice of him. Defensive line coach Charlie Partridge recalled his young defensive lineman was a "tweener" when he first arrived, as Hemer weighed only 240 to 250 pounds.

He was inexperienced with football due to a focus on other sports like hockey, but he had a big frame and room to grow in the weight room and on the field.

"He came in and just worked," Partridge said bluntly.

Ethan Hemer (87) bats down a Northern Iowa pass attempt. | AP Photo

Most notably, the starting offensive line began to know his name, but not in the way that would make him any friends. Hemer was a thorn in the side of the offensive line as a member of the defensive scout team.

"It's 90 degrees out and we're in Camp Randall practicing," former Wisconsin and current Cincinnati Bengals guard Kevin Zeitler recalled, laughing. "We have 35 plays to run the first day in fall camp, and he decides to be the 'Scout Team Hero' – a.k.a. a guy who goes all out every play. The starters hate those guys. Thirty plays in, we're all dying on the o-line, and he's still making plays and (offensive line coach Bob) Bostad went off on us."

Hemer earned Defensive Scout Team Player of the Year honors in 2009. It was his goal that season, as J.J. Watt received that distinction the prior year and had progressed to a starting role the following season.

Hemer's ascent continued as he cracked the two-deep on

the defensive depth-chart heading into the 2010 season, backing up starters Patrick Butrym and Jordan Kohout. Many noticed the dedication and drive from the walk-on.

"When I first met Hemer, I thought he was a little goofy. There weren't many quite like him. After a couple of months, I loved the kid," former defensive end and current Wisconsin graduate assistant Pat Muldoon acknowledged. "He's such a good hearted kid and so hard working. The transition from when he first walked on campus to starting as a redshirt freshman was insane. He grew so much as a player and a person."

Hemer saw action in all 13 games that year, and when Kohout suffered an injury against No. 1 Ohio State, Hemer filled in with four tackles in that 31-18 upset win. The Medford product would make the first of six starts against Iowa, and like Ewing and Watt, he delivered in Iowa City – registering what would be a career-high six stops.

The walk-on finished the year with 21 tackles, was a consistent starter, and thought he had done enough to earn a scholarship.

Enter Russell Wilson.

With the quarterback's arrival to Wisconsin, Hemer would not receive a scholarship until January 2012. Although no bitterness remains, he admitted he briefly entertained the idea of looking around at other programs.

Loyalty to the team he grew up admiring kept him in Madison.

"Just being a part of what Wisconsin was and what it represented," Hemer said as his reason for staying at UW. "Being a part of the team meant more to me than going to another school and getting a scholarship and playing. I was playing at UW. The only thing I didn't have was the monthly checks. I knew that I was good enough to play at that level – I had shown it on the field, I had shown it in the classroom. I was doing everything the right way, and it was just a matter of time. It wasn't if, it was just when.

"Talking with my coach, mentors, teammates, and guys that graduated – I realized this was home. This is where I was supposed to be, where I was meant to be.

"I knew I had done enough to earn a scholarship, but due to certain circumstances I couldn't have it. But I was doing something that was bigger than just me. I was a part of something that meant more than just being a scholarship kid. I'm glad I made that decision to stay and stick it out because I was a part of some really great teams and have some really great memories."

In 2011, he started all 14 games and contributed a career-high 34 tackles for the Badgers. Hemer's perseverance and work ethic on the field and in the weight room was admirable, but he was also known for his enjoyable personality.

"I could always count on one of the players listening to music when I came back to my office," Partridge recalled. "I would have Pandora on, and Ethan was always the one putting some stupid channel on and turning the volume all the way up. He put Donna Summers on there one time and cranked it up or Backstreet Boys or something stupid. That's his sense of humor."

Partridge would coach Hemer until the 2013 Rose Bowl, a 20-14 loss to the Stanford Cardinal, before both he and co-defensive coordinator Chris Ash would leave to join Bielema at Arkansas.

New head coach Gary Andersen switched defensive schemes to a 3-4 alignment. It would be the first of two major transitions Hemer would again have to face. He wasn't just learning a new defense under new coordinator Dave Aranda, but he'd also have to acclimate physically.

All of this, during what would be his final year of eligibility.

"Up to that point Beau Allen and myself had kind of solidified our positions," said Hemer, who would play a big, space-eating "three" technique (aligned outside the guard) and "one" technique (aligned outside of the center) in the previous 4-3 defense. "We're looking to have great senior years in a familiar defense and that all changed. The first day that Andersen was in at the office, I went in there and asked him, 'Where do I fit in this scheme?'"

The new head coach assured him he would be a key member of the defense, but wanted Hemer to play defensive end, lining up directly across from the tackle.

Hemer would have to work with a new defensive line coach in Chad Kau'aha'aha. Coming from Utah, there was an adjustment for both the players and position coach in Aranda's 3-4 scheme. Hemer would also have to compete for playing time with teammates like Muldoon, Tyler Dippel and Konrad Zagzebski, all defensive ends in the previous scheme.

The coaching staff also wanted Hemer to lose weight. He recalls weighing around 315 to 320 pounds as a defensive tackle, but would drop down to 290 with the position change. His weight got as low as 285 during the season.

"You can imagine how drastic of a change that is," Hemer said. "You go from strong, tough, and then drop a bunch of weight. I can run forever but I felt I lost strength. It was so drastic of a change in such a short time that I was very frustrated with the results."

"It was a big change," Borland acknowledged, "especially going into his senior season with a guy who has potential to play professionally, and the coaching staff asked a lot of him. But he bucked up, and that just shows the type of guy he is."

Like the scholarship situation when Wilson arrived, or his stint on the scout team, Hemer always put the team before himself.

He played in all 13 of his final collegiate games, including eight starts. Wisconsin's defense finished in the top ten in the FBS in four key defensive categories. The new scheme allowed Hemer to expand his horizons in techniques and alignments.

"Looking back, I'm very thankful I went through that because it taught me how to deal with difficult situations," Hemer, who was on the practice squad of the Pittsburgh Steelers during the 2014 season, recalled. "I know a ton more about football because I know more about positions and what to expect out of people in different defenses."

From 2010-13 when Hemer contributed on the field, his

teams finished with 39 total wins during one of the most successful four year periods in school history.

"He's all about Wisconsin football, and he was going to do anything he could to help this team win," Armstrong acknowledged.

"He was just so unselfish and the best guy to have in the locker room. He could get along with anybody and everybody. If you have a team full of those guys, you're going to be successful."

****

The bond between players runs deep at Wisconsin. A trip to a teammate's hometown usually makes for a great getaway from the constant conditioning and training.

Such was the case in the summer of 2013. Twelve Badgers – among them Hemer, Armstrong, Borland and Muldoon – kayaked and fished on a hot afternoon near Ottawa, Ill. As they made their way back into town they stumbled upon an ice cream shop called Tone's Cones and its "Tone's Belt Buster Challenge."

Ethan Armstrong (36) chases down Northwestern quarterback Kain Colter. | AP Photo

The Belt Buster Challenge was a monstrous, frozen concoction of sweetness containing two quarts of ice cream, 10 helpings of toppings all covered with a can of whipped cream. It was a dessert Armstrong lovingly described as a "disgusting amount of food." The lucky, or unlucky, contestant would have only 20 minutes to devour it, with a free meal, T-shirt, and picture on the Tone's Hall of Fame hanging in the balance.

The players convinced Hemer to take on the challenge by agreeing to pay the fee if he could not eat it all.

The theme from *Rocky* blasted through the air as the defensive lineman attacked the mounds of ice cream, like Sly Stallone attacking Apollo Creed.

Unfortunately, the Belt Buster Challenge didn't end well for Hemer. Armstrong felt the defensive end made a strategic error by picking hard candy as his toppings instead of going with a softer topping like hot fudge.

"It was a very noble effort, but it ended with him throwing up ice cream in the garbage can," Armstrong conceded.

To add insult to stomach injury...

"We bought extra cans of whipped cream to celebrate his victory, because we thought for sure he was going to destroy it," Armstrong continued. "When he lost, we were all disappointed, but we still had this extra whipped cream that we needed to use. So while he's throwing up in the garbage can, we just started spraying him with the whipped cream anyway."

A hero's triumph it was not. Hemer would be in a self-described food "coma" until later that evening.

Ottawa is a small city of 18,000-plus where Armstrong grew up before moving on to play 52 games for the Badgers. The linebacker started the final 27 games of his collegiate career from 2012-13.

What makes his story special is the fact that he missed only two of 54 possible games despite having ten surgeries in his five years in Madison.

Ten operations: three on his knees, three on his shoulders,

three on his hips, plus one to repair a dislocated thumb and torn UCL ligament. The appendage was detached and dangling after Wisconsin's 33-29 heartbreaking loss to Ohio State on October 29, 2011.

"It was just kind of hanging there," Armstrong said with a nostalgic laugh about the hand injury. "It was pretty ugly. We ended up doing surgery on Monday, and then I was practicing that Tuesday. They just clubbed it up, covered the pins up, and I was back at practice."

He didn't miss a game though, recording five tackles and a pass breakup in a 62-17 blowout win against Purdue at home the following week.

Throughout his time at Wisconsin, he only participated in one series of spring practices, his redshirt freshman year in 2010, due to rehabbing injuries. Call him Wisconsin's equivalent of the famed Marvel Comics character, Iron Man. He got knocked down, rebuilt himself, and returned to the field.

"I really appreciated his love of the game. As a walk-on, to go through all the sacrifices with his body while still paying for school was tough," said linebacker Derek Landisch, who saw firsthand the hurdles Armstrong faced as his roommate. "The culture of Wisconsin is that when you suit up you play for Wisconsin, you don't play for yourself. He embodied that."

Armstrong's and Borland's close friendship strengthened when both were recovering from shoulder injuries during the spring of 2011. Their 5:30 a.m. lifting sessions with then-strength and conditioning coach Ben Herbert pushed each other back onto the field. After the hip surgeries, Armstrong also fused a strong friendship with fellow linebacker Mike Taylor, who himself was going through rehabilitation for a similar injury.

That linebacking trio would also go through many changes with their position coach. It's not uncommon to have some transition or turnover in the college game, but Borland and Armstrong endured four different position coaches in their time at Wisconsin. Armstrong and Borland also flip-flopped at inside and outside linebackers in the 4-3 scheme after their first two seasons. Armstrong further transitioned to a 3-4 outside linebacker when Aranda arrived.

"The coaching change is difficult but everything that Wisconsin wants out of their players – smart, tough, dependable – allows you to handle those transitions," Armstrong said. "You have to listen and respect what your coach has to say, you have to go out and execute, and there are no excuses. You have to get your job done."

Endurance through these stressful situations is a key characteristic for the "Iron Man." Herbert mentally pushed players in conditioning drills, pitting them against each other to simulate their opponents on the field. Armstrong's work ethic didn't go unnoticed during the many tests Herbert dished out.

"He was such a tough dude," linebacker Marcus Trotter stated. "I don't think I've met someone as mentally tough as him. There would be workouts where the workout would be specifically designed to make everyone fall down, and he's the only one still standing. I've admired him since day one."

"There were some pretty legendary workouts," Armstrong snickered. "We would go up and climb the upper decks of Camp Randall Stadium carrying 100 pound or 75 pound sandbags on our shoulders, or pushing 600-pound prowler sleds across the field, or even just the simple drills where you're competing against the guy across from you. The loser had to come in the next morning at 5 a.m. to get a shake – there was always something on the line and that created a competitive edge that those teams carried."

That work ethic and extra heartbeat, as Bielema believed many walk-ons like Armstrong had, led him to start 29 total games in his career. He finished third on the team in tackles his final two seasons with 51 and 93 stops, respectively. He also had the opportunity to play with his brother, Thaddeus, a backup quarterback and fellow walk-on.

For his efforts in his time at Wisconsin, Armstrong was awarded the Jay Seiler Coaches Appreciation Award in 2012, given to the "defensive player who has contributed to the team's success to the best of his abilities." He was also named UW's Comeback Player of the Year his senior season, returning from left shoulder surgery in the spring.

Those who played alongside Armstrong have the utmost admiration for him.

"I don't know if I have more respect for anyone in the world," Borland proudly said. "Really smart guy, extremely hard-working. He faced and overcame as much adversity as any player that I've played with."

****

"The whole time I was on the sideline thinking about an exam. 'Did I get 'A' wrong or 'B' wrong?'"

That was the thought process inside Marcus Trotter's mind in Champaign, Ill., on October 19, 2013.

In his defense, up to that point Trotter had only played in nine games the previous two seasons despite working his way into the two-deep during his redshirt sophomore year. On top of that, he was behind the freakishly talented Chris Borland.

Playing time was hard to come by.

But when the 2013 Big Ten Linebacker of the Year suffered a hamstring injury covering a punt in the first quarter against the Fighting Illini, Trotter heard his name being yelled.

"I thought, 'What the hell?'" Trotter laughed, "and next thing I know, I'm in the game at inside linebacker making calls."

He finished the game as Wisconsin's leading tackler with nine stops in the 56-32 win, but the true test came the next week against Iowa on the road. The Racine native was set to make his first of 13 career starts in Iowa City.

"I was super pumped," recalled Trotter, who was notified he would start during pregame drills. "I was born and raised a huge Iowa fan. I loved the colors, I loved the Iowa Hawkeyes. For me to go against them was a dream come true."

According to Trotter, he suffered a torn hip flexor on the fifth or sixth play of the game, but he wouldn't let that hamper him from contributing. He once again led the team with nine tackles, including one-and-a-half for loss in a 28-9 win. He also forced a key interception when he blitzed, forcing Iowa quarterback C.J. Beathard to make an errant throw in a 14-9 game. The result was a quick Badger score that put the game out of reach.

Marcus Trotter (59) would become a full-time starter at linebacker during the 2014 season. | AP Photo

Like many walk-ons when given the chance on the field, Trotter shined. His play in 2013 would allow him to become a dependable full-time starter in 2014. He led the Chevy Bad Boyz – the energetic group of linebackers that dominated the stat sheets – on the way to UW's first bowl win in over five years.

It was a long road with many obstacles in his path, but Trotter developed into a consistent contributor and one of the most charismatic faces Wisconsin has seen in recent memory.

"Being able to see him from his senior year in high school to his senior year in college, mature and grow into a leadership position," Armstrong said, "to watch his personality blossom, it was neat to see him become more comfortable and let his personality carry him. He always played to his strengths and he was very much an intellectual player."

Just getting the opportunity to get on the field in a consistent manner was a long journey. The same can be said about his recruiting process. His twin brother, Michael, was a prep standout at Marquette High School and ranked the top player in Wisconsin, according to Rivals.com. He also earned the state's Defensive Player of the Year award. Both were three-star talents, but Michael was seeing the light shine on him more.

That was evident one day in the Hilltopper weight room when their legendary coach, Dick Basham, came in and told Michael he received a scholarship offer from the Badgers. While Michael was ecstatic, Marcus wasn't offered and dealt with a melancholy situation. The brothers were inseparable and best friends.

"I was heartbroken," Trotter conceded, who noted many schools balked at his slow 40-yard dash time. "I will never forget that moment, I remember the feeling I had inside that I was going to prove everyone wrong. It's kind of cliché, but it was like a fire in myself."

Trotter would receive scholarship offers from Northern Iowa, Illinois State, Wofford and even a late one from Western Michigan. He admitted feeling like he wasn't offered more because many coaching staffs believed the brothers would be a package deal – where Michael would go, so would Marcus.

A prime example came from a Big Ten school recruiting the brothers. Marcus received an offer from the school, but acknowledged it was mostly done to get his brother to commit along with him. Michael remembered the school even wrote a handwritten letter to both, noting they were the only ones who offered the twins and trying to leverage that opportunity.

One evening, Marcus spoke with the team's coaches, but they also wanted to speak with their main target, Michael. Michael was away, so Marcus disguised himself vocally in a way only a twin brother can.

"So I was acting like myself and I said, 'Hold on, here's Michael.' I literally covered the phone for five seconds, changed my voice, and they bought it," Marcus said. "They literally told me, 'Marcus is okay, but we really need you.'"

"I couldn't play for a program that didn't want me."

Michael committed to Wisconsin in July 2009, but Marcus was still weighing his options. Minnesota threw in a late walk-on offer, and Marcus made a last-minute trip to the Twin Cities with his father without telling anyone. He even came home with a Minnesota cap on, but ultimately decided to join his brother at UW.

There were also family ties to Madison. Their sister, Alana played basketball at Wisconsin from 2007-10 and would be a senior when they were freshmen. On a somber note, their older brother, Aleksas, a former Penn State gymnastics standout, committed suicide in Madison in April 2008. The tragedy bonded the once-quarreling twins to this day, and Marcus was drawn to live and play in Madison.

"I've always had this weird connection with that," Trotter conceded, "so I've always told myself, if I was going to make it big somewhere, I would rather go somewhere my brother used to live."

Pushing through the depth charts would also be a years-long struggle. With a chip on his shoulder and resisting the notion of moving to fullback, he redshirted his first season. Hamstring injuries derailed his redshirt freshman campaign in 2011, playing mostly on special teams in five games while being relegated again to scout-team duty.

2012 would allow both Trotters to move up the depth chart. Michael started three games while playing in 13. Marcus found himself backing up Borland at middle linebacker in the 4-3 defense.

Marcus would have his moments in Gary Andersen's first year in 2013, but the following season is where he found himself in a larger, more prominent role. Gone would be Borland, who was drafted in the third round by the San Francisco 49ers in the 2014 NFL Draft. The former walk-on would get his chance to start and let loose his alter-ego, "Mookie," a nickname he was given early in his high school years while playing video games.

All of the returning linebackers, for that matter, would get a chance to showcase their abilities. Borland, Armstrong, Brendan Kelly, and Conor O'Neill exhausted their eligibility and moved on from the college game. Insert Trotter, Landisch, Vince Biegel, and Joe Schobert. Though the stats showed they had few starts under their belts, all found roles within defensive coordinator Dave Aranda's defense.

The pieces were in place, but according to Trotter, it took until the October 25 game against Maryland for the Chevy Bad Boyz to assert themselves.

In that 52-7 win, Wisconsin's defense suffocated a Maryland offense allowing just 175 total offensive yards, with the starting linebackers contributing 20 tackles and 6.5 tackles for loss. Four of the linebacking crew – Marcus, Schobert, Jack Cichy and Ben Ruechel – were walk-ons.

Their nickname developed as a variation on what former co-defensive coordinator Chris Ash used to call his players in the defensive backfield – the Badger Bad Boys.

"I was bored one day, and I was thinking, 'I like the Bad Boyz part, but what could I change besides the Badger?'" Trotter laughed. "Well, all of our linebackers like country. They like Miller High Life and guitars and all that stuff. That's just swag, so I thought it was only right to be called the Chevy Bad Boyz."

The defense was in good hands and didn't miss a beat. The starting four were in the top-six of the Badgers' leading tacklers, and all registered double digit tackles for loss. Trotter ended up second on the team in tackles with 93 along with 12 tackles for loss. His imprint on the program was noticeable on the field but amplified by the off-the-wall conversations at the dinner table with the linebackers group.

"You can't believe half of what Marcus says, but that's just him, and he's great for it. He told tall tales of who I idolized in high school," said Landisch who played against the Trotters' Hilltoppers in high school. "He would always say, 'True or false, you had a picture of me on your mirror and worked out trying to beat me like in the Rocky movie.'"

"Mookie" led Wisconsin's defense to another banner performance in their second season under Aranda. The squad ranked fourth in the nation in total defense, allowing 294.1 yards per game, fourth nationally in passing defense (168.0 yards per game) and finished 17th nationally in scoring defense (20.8 points per game). Despite Andersen bolting to Oregon State just days after their 59-0 Big Ten Championship game loss to Ohio State, the team bonded under Alvarez, who became acting head coach. Trotter recorded eight tackles, one for loss, in the 34-31 victory over Auburn in the Outback Bowl.

It was a fitting end to Trotter's career. He now attends medical school at Indiana University, but the mark he left at Wisconsin combines his on-the-field success, his infectious personality, and his drive to succeed that was characteristic of the UW walk-on tradition.

All he needed was that chance.

"Back in high school, I was really big into looking at forums, and recruiting chat boards. I can't tell you how many times I read, 'He's not good enough, he'll never play a down. He's not fast enough. He should be a fullback.'

"There's nothing better than proving people wrong, because it felt like 100 people told me I couldn't do it, and for some reason in the back of my mind I felt like I could. I'm just glad Coach Andersen gave me that opportunity."

****

For the natural charisma Trotter displayed on and off the field, former safety Joe Stellmacher would be considered at the opposite end of the spectrum.

Teammates recall "Stelli" as a very mild-mannered student-athlete but the small-town Stellmacher brought an edge that got him on the field early and often in the mid-2000s. His football intelligence covered up a lack of top-end speed in the defensive backfield. His mental astuteness was a common trait many pointed out.

"He was like Jimmy (Leonhard) in a lot of ways," acknowledged left tackle Joe Thomas, who was named team MVP with Stellmacher and four other seniors after their 12-1 season in 2006. "He was a really smart guy back there in the secondary."

"He would key in on things that guys would give away with routes. Honestly, I don't think I ever got Joe on a double move, ever, because he was patient enough to wait on it and not commit himself to the first move I put on," tight end Owen Daniels acknowledged.

Unlike those who received scholarship offers from Division II schools or FCS programs, Stellmacher only visited three college campuses – Ripon, Wisconsin-La Crosse and Madison – before deciding to walk-on to UW despite being a first-team all-state selection by the WFCA, AP, and the *Milwaukee Journal Sentinel.*

Unlike Trotter, Thompson and many others, the lack of college recruiters didn't give Stellmacher a chip on his shoulder. Stellmacher admitted if he could get a sniff of the field at Wisconsin in any role, he'd be a happy camper.

More was in store for him, though, after redshirting his first year in 2002, he began to climb the depth chart in the spring of 2003 with the help of some injuries in the secondary.

Despite his head spinning that first year, the game began to slow down for him with increased reps during spring practices. It would prep him for a larger role in the fall as the starting nickel back, the fifth defensive back employed during obvious passing downs.

Stellmacher's first game experience came on the rowdy campus of Morgantown, West Virginia, when Wisconsin traveled to face the Mountaineers in their season opener.

"We're on the bus, and all of a sudden, the street is just lined with kids. I remember them banging on the bus and yelling at us. I was like, 'Holy crap, is this what college ball is all about?'" Stellmacher laughed.

The Badgers would prevail in the non-conference battle with Stellmacher tallying his first two tackles of his collegiate career. He went on to contribute significantly in the team's next five games, including six tackles in UW's 48-31 shootout victory against Akron.

His hard work was rewarded with his first start against UNLV, where despite contributing five tackles (1.5 for loss) and helping hold the Rebels to 187 total offensive yards, UW lost in disappointing fashion, 23-5. His rise up the ranks would come to a halt, unfortunately, as he broke his leg in a 38-20 win over Illinois.

It took two seasons for Stellmacher to get back into the starting fold, but he played in 12 games in 2004, mostly in a reserve and special team's role.

Despite starting second on the depth chart behind junior Johnny White entering 2005, Stellmacher's aggressiveness helped bump him back up to the first-team defense in the second game of the season against Temple.

"Joe was a real tough guy and he was a pretty big hitter," Thomas said. "He had to have a linebacker's mentality for being sort of undersized at safety, even more so than Jimmy."

That gritty, physical nature was evident in Wisconsin's 23-20 win over Michigan in the conference opener in late September. On the Wolverines' first offensive series, Stellmacher collided with running back Kevin Grady, suffering a stinger. He'd go to the sideline, but only temporarily.

As the Wolverines drove 94 yards on that series, a 4th-and-goal situation at the one-yard line arose. Rather than taking the three points to take the lead, Michigan head coach Lloyd Carr decided to hand the rock to Grady once again. Stellmacher, back in the game, stopped Grady's

Joe Stellmacher (16) unloads on Michigan receiver Adrian Arrington (16). | AP Photo

momentum – helping the Badgers make a goal-line stand.

He paired with Roderick Rogers to create a formidable defensive backfield from 2005-06, finishing second in tackles his final two years.

Despite overtures from those who believed he could make it in the NFL, Stellmacher didn't pursue playing on Sundays. Rather, he stayed in the family business of coaching, as his father, Steve, coached Joe in high school.

Stellmacher would begin at UW as a quality control assistant in 2007. He found his way back to Berlin for the 2010 prep season as an assistant, then took over the head coaching reins the following season.

Instilling the principles he saw Alvarez utilize at Wisconsin, he rebuilt the program. In the past two seasons, Stellmacher has guided Berlin to two state playoff berths and a 9-2 overall record in 2015.

"Being a walk-on, you gotta work for everything," Stellmacher said. "Nothing's going to be handed to you. That's the approach I've taken into my coaching career."

CHAPTER EIGHT

Embracing the Opportunity

Paul Hubbard was drafted in the sixth round of the 2008 draft by the Cleveland Browns following a Wisconsin career in which he caught 53 receptions for 936 yards and five touchdowns. He ended up playing for four NFL franchises throughout his professional career.

Hubbard came to UW on a track scholarship to compete for the legendary Ed Nuttycombe, but Alvarez also recruited him to play football. A rule was in place dictating he could not play in a game if he was on a track scholarship, so he worked with the scout team while learning the position.

During the 2003 season, he captured the Big Ten Conference indoor and outdoor long jump championships, while placing fourth in the indoor triple jump. Though there were accolades in track, he wanted to continue playing football.

Henry Mason, his former position coach, noted it took some time for Hubbard to develop and mentally switch over from a track to football-focused mentality. The wake-up call came while watching UW great Lee Evans haul in the game-winning, 79-yard touchdown catch from Matt Schabert in the 17-10 upset over No. 3 Ohio State in 2003.

"I'm thinking to myself, if I was in that situation, could I have been able to do that, on that stage, knowing all that was riding on that play?" Hubbard questioned. "I thought to myself, 'Man, I have a lot more work to do.'"

From that point on, he dedicated himself to improving his

craft at wide receiver. With all of his speed and athleticism, Hubbard would have to work on his concentration. His tendency to take his eyes off the ball and look up the field before catching a potential pass hindered his effectiveness as a receiver. Mason instituted a new rule according to Hubbard: 25 push-ups for every dropped ball. After one practice where focus was lacking, drops piled up. So did the extra push-ups – around 125 total – but it was all done in hope of replicating some of the big plays made by Evans and the other talented receivers ahead of him on the depth chart.

Paul Hubbard (19) hauls in a catch for a big gain against Indiana corner Tracy Porter (9). | AP Photo

After spring practices in 2004, Hubbard's scholarship was transferred to football, and his efforts to improve on the field rewarded. The opportunity allowed him to see the field consistently, and ultimately reach his goal as a go-to receiver.

His journey, like Swan's, would take three years. Mason acknowledged they may have tried to throw too much at the relatively inexperienced Hubbard, as the Colorado native didn't play football until later in his adolescence. After the coaches trimmed down what they were asking him to do, he began making strides in his performance.

He ascended with Swan to the first-team offense, as the former walk-ons formed quite a duo during Bielema's first season as head coach in 2006.

Starting all 13 games, Hubbard caught 38 passes for 627 yards, good for second on the team in both categories, while tying Swan for the team lead in touchdown receptions (five). His track background helped him become that big-play target for Chryst and his offense, averaging 16.5 yards per catch. Though 2007 would be a struggle – as a knee injury would keep him out five games and restrict his contributions (14 catches, 305 yards) – the multi-sport athlete found his niche in Wisconsin's offense.

****

Some walk-ons, like Hubbard, worked their way up to be first-team and greatly contribute to the overall success of the team. Others waited for their moments to contribute. Whether injuries, suspensions or poor play by teammates, they stepped up and delivered when their number was called. Many knew their respective roles and devoted themselves to ensuring the program's success whenever possible.

Just a year prior to Hubbard's arrival in Madison, David Braun finished his last season in a Wisconsin uniform. He turned down walk-on offers from Minnesota and Iowa to join UW after being named second-team all-state by the Associated Press and the *Milwaukee Journal Sentinel*. In 1999, he was behind Chris Chambers and Conroy Whyte as the third split end, or what was known as the "X" wide receiver. In 2000 and 2001, he moved to flanker, the "Z" receiver," and could spell both Davis and Evans if called upon.

For Braun, like many working their way through the

depth chart, special teams opened the door for him to gain playing time on offense. He rose up through the ranks as a redshirt freshman on the second of back-to-back Rose Bowl championship seasons.

"We were practicing special teams, going all out, and I remember I just pancake-blocked a player. It was filmed just right so assistant coach John Palermo kept asking, 'Who is this?' The next day, I was on all special teams as a redshirt freshman."

Braun played in 10 games and contributed on three units that year – kickoff, kickoff return and punt return – as the Badgers won their second straight conference title and trip to Pasadena. It was a pleasant change compared to sitting at home for away games or getting pummeled by Doering and Co. as a scout team body his redshirt year in 1998.

He caught only two passes that year, but Braun emerged with an important reception to end the 2000 season against UCLA in the Sun Bowl. In the fourth quarter, the Madison native hauled in a Bollinger pass that would move the chains on a 3rd-and-5 from the Bruins' 11-yard line. Bennett would take it in from six yards out to tie the game the next play. The extra point would give the Badgers a 21-20 victory.

His greatest game as a wide receiver, however, came two years later. With his former travel buddy Evans sidelined for the year with a significant knee injury, he was named the team's offensive player of the week in a narrow 24-21 victory over Northern Illinois. As the Huskies stormed back to take a 21-17 lead late in the fourth quarter, Wisconsin got the ball back at midfield with 2:13 left in the game.

On the first play of the drive, Braun snagged an 8-yard reception to the Huskies' 42, and later, caught an 18-yard pass from Bollinger to give the Badgers a first down at the NIU 14. The very next play, the veteran UW signal caller again called the former walk-on's number to help put Wisconsin up for good.

"I thought I was going to score that touchdown right at the goal line," Braun remembered with a laugh, "but the guy – it wasn't a glaringly obvious pass interference, but he did hook my hip because I was diving to catch it. Their coaches went nuts and thought it was a homer job, but it was a pass interference."

Bollinger took it in from two yards for the go-ahead touchdown, and Wisconsin would escape with a three-point victory. Braun would catch four passes for 56 yards against the Huskies that Saturday, and nine overall for the season. Stepping up in a critical fashion on offense wasn't surprising, according to his former position coach.

"One thing that stood out was that everything that you coached him to do, he did it," Mason recollected. "His steps, he was at the right place at the right time, and the quarterback could depend upon him. He was able to step in and play in any situation."

****

Dreams of a third consecutive Rose Bowl and Big Ten championship may have changed due to the Shoe Box scandal, but one thing didn't between 1999 and 2000: the chant of "MATT-U-NER-TL" by fans throughout Camp Randall Stadium on Saturdays.

He was a reserve running back who, like Panos before him, transferred to UW from a Division III school in Wisconsin. Unertl's name began to make its way through the stands after Dayne eclipsed the NCAA all-time rushing record against Iowa during the 1999 season. The UW public address announcer, Mike Mahnke, routinely would decry to the jam-packed sections of fans, "Ron Dayne!" after each carry.

When Dayne was pulled from the dominating 41-3 victory over Iowa, Unertl (pronounced you-NER-tel) got the bulk of the carries on Wisconsin's final offensive series. The former UW-La Crosse running back carried the ball seven times that drive. As UW drove towards the student section, "MATT U-NER-TL" was chanted by those in the stands.

"We get to the 30-yard line, and the offensive line starters were still in the game. They're like, 'Are you hearing this?'"

Unertl remembered, noting he acknowledged the chants but tried not to get distracted.

"As we're getting closer and closer, it's getting louder and louder. It's funny because I was trying to stay focused and get back in the huddle, but my offensive linemen loved it."

The Sussex, Wis., native became a fan favorite, mostly receiving playing time on special teams and in clean-up duty during blowouts early on. With Dayne gone in that 2000 season, two games defined his role as a viable and hard-nosed back that the coaching staff could rely upon when others faulted, especially in tough contests against conference foes.

Wisconsin faced Minnesota on Senior Day. Michael Bennett hadn't received a single carry all game due to injury, but UW had gone up 27-20 after a Bollinger touchdown run. The Badgers took over on offense following a Gophers turnover.

With reserve running back Eddie Faulkner out with a concussion, Unertl would see Bollinger hand the ball off into his gut seven times to secure the lead.

"I knew since I didn't get as much time to carry the ball, that when I did get in there, I had to take full advantage," Unertl explained.

Matt Unertl (38) became a fan favorite during his time at Wisconsin. | Wisconsin State Journal

"Sometimes it creates a little more sense of urgency."

In a drive that personified Wisconsin's no-nonsense, power running game, Unertl gained 32 yards on those seven carries on a mixture of zone blocks and power runs orchestrated by the dominant Wisconsin offensive line. After each carry, Unertl's name was cheered by the crowd.

"The next drive, (running backs coach Brian White) must have been feeling the running game and we just clipped off five, six, seven, eight yards a carry on those drives and kept the drive going," Unertl stated, as UW ate up four minutes, 39 seconds on the clock. "It was like a slow machine moving. It was kind of crazy being Senior Day. It was just funny how it all worked out."

With the crowd eagerly awaiting Unertl's name being called one last time, he took the handoff from Bollinger. He forced his way into the end zone through a mound of players for a one-yard score. Badgers fans erupted as they extended their lead against their rivals to a two-score advantage, and with a late pick-six by cornerback Mike Echols, Wisconsin won 41-20.

The week after, UW traveled to Bloomington to face the Hoosiers. Unertl provided a durable running option on the afternoon, gaining 59 yards on 12 carries in a 43-22 win. On the field, he was a bruiser, a solid back-up and a reliable ball carrier. From his Division III beginnings at UW-La Crosse, he found his niche in the Wisconsin backfield.

****

Like Unertl, Appleton's Kyle Zuleger was an in-state kid who played a key reserve role for the Badgers. Both were running backs, but unlike the Sussex native, Zuleger's contributions at tailback wouldn't increase over his time at Wisconsin.

In fact, seven of his last eight career carries came during his redshirt freshman season in 2010. That shouldn't come as a surprise, however, when you consider the depth the position had during those successful years with John Clay,

Montee Ball, James White and Melvin Gordon ahead of him.

With freshman Corey Clement incoming and Vonte Jackson returning from injury, Coach Gary Andersen asked Zuleger to switch over to safety in the spring of 2013 to provide stability in the defensive backfield. He wouldn't necessarily make his mark on either side of the ball, but he played in 52 career games as a key member of the Badgers' special teams units.

It takes a certain type of person to make a living in this phase of the game. Like many walk-ons before him, he took on whatever the program asked of him, and made it work to his advantage. He also understood the importance of the units he would later lead.

"For me, my mentality was to simply play faster than everybody else on the field. I'm not necessarily the fastest, but I got afterburners when I need it," Zuleger laughed. "For me it was to play fast and to have a reckless abandon that was controlled. Special teams is a hundred miles per hour. It's a very unique part of the game because your biggest momentum swings arguably come in special teams."

Zuleger was part of that great class of 2009 that churned out prominent walk-ons like Hemer, Armstrong and Abbrederis. The Appleton East High School graduate redshirted that first year, but found his niche on the kickoff team in his first career game against UNLV. He recorded two tackles and was named co-special team's player of the week for those efforts. It would lead to a much greater presence on the team, though not necessarily the most glamorous.

"I was doing pretty good, mostly because I was hyped up on adrenaline running down on kickoff coverage, disrupting everything that (our opponents) had going on, which allowed the rest of the coverage team to do well that game. As a result, the coaches expanded my role and from the very first game, it was a steady crescendo. I started going on to more coverage teams, and by the end of my freshman to my senior year, I was on all four special teams units getting nearly 30 reps per game."

Zuleger may be the true definition of what a "glue guy" is

Kyle Zuleger (27) brings down Ohio State running back Dontre Wilson (1). | AP Photo

for a Division I college football program and was an example of a player who embraced his role as a special teams ace. He created his opportunities and made the most of his chances when presented. It paid off, as he would be one of the team's captains during a couple of games of the 2013 season (unlike previous years, captains would be named for each game).

"He was one of those critical guys that Wisconsin could always count on, whether he was blocking, whether he was a gunner. Whatever Wisconsin needed him to do, he was willing to do it," BadgerNation.com's Ben Worgull said. "He just did it because he loved playing football, he loved playing for Wisconsin, and he took pride in his small role to the best of his ability."

"At the end of my career, I think coaches and teammates saw me as an experienced special team's ace," Zuleger said. "I was able to have the opportunity to return kicks and have different roles for special teams with specific game plans for opponents – mainly because I had such a deep run on those units and was very well educated on each position on each unit."

Zuleger never became a household name like fellow walk-ons Leonhard, Watt, or Abbrederis. It didn't, however, deter him from going out and competing every day for five years. He recorded 36 career tackles, including a career-high five against Purdue in 2013, and earned some significant accolades as a Badger.

"I wanted to get my playing time at running back, but I was still getting just as many reps as everybody else through special teams. More importantly, we were winning. As time went on, I realized my role was going to be on special teams, so in my mind, I said, 'If that's what it's going to be, I'm going to be the best at it.' Fortunately, I was able to earn my scholarship for my last two years. My junior and senior year, I was Special Teams Player of the Year. Whatever we were doing, it was working – and I was happy."

****

Zach Hampton donned the cardinal and white uniform as a four-year letter winner from 2003-06. In those 42 games he played, he rolled up his sleeves and made his mark primarily on special teams. Like Zuleger, he initially started off on the kickoff team his redshirt freshman year then later expanded his repertoire to all four major coverage units, including being named the premier punt returner his final season.

For the Lancaster, Wis., native, however, his star shined brightest in his last game as a student athlete.

On January 1, 2007, the Badgers faced the Arkansas Razorbacks in the Capital One Bowl in Orlando. In the second quarter, starting free safety Roderick Rogers went down with a right knee injury. Hampton, who floated between cornerback and safety during his career, stepped in and delivered his best defensive performance of his career, recording five tackles, an interception and knocking down the Razorbacks' final pass to secure UW's 17-14 win.

Hampton's initial role was on the other side of the ball when he first came to Madison, though. After being named first-team all-state by the Associated Press and WFCA as well as the Small School Player of the Year by the *Wisconsin State Journal* in both his junior and senior years, he started off his collegiate career as a wide receiver. It wasn't the right fit, however.

"I couldn't really tell you why I chose to start out at receiver," Hampton admitted. "It was probably not the right choice, to be honest with you. I think I had a better chance to get on the field when I moved to defense."

He floundered through a deep receiving corps that boasted Williams, Orr, and Darrin Charles as regulars that first year in 2002.

The start of the 2003 campaign didn't fare well, as he initially received some attention in special teams in the spring but was soon passed over. Still struggling to get noticed, he would finally get his opportunity when Alvarez held open tryouts on the kickoff unit. According to Hampton, he made three consecutive stops during the special teams' scrimmage. He earned his spot.

"I finally had my chance," Hampton said. "I was traveling with the team, and that was what basically turned everything around for me."

Though he wasn't credited with game action in that 2003 upset win over Ohio State in October, he noted he was on the field on the opening kickoff and was in on the first tackle as part of the kickoff coverage unit. That year also signified a change in his position as he'd head over to the defensive secondary.

An opportunity to work behind and learn from another All-American in Leonhard, and the chance to see some playing time outside of coverage units highly appealed to him.

"That was actually the coaches' decision to bring me over to defense," Hampton said. "We were lacking a little bit of depth at the safety position. I didn't get any playing time, specifically because I was behind Jim, but I was just better suited on the defensive side."

He enhanced his special teams resume in the following years, contributing in the punt return, punt, and kickoff return coverage teams. That dedication would pay off when he was awarded the 2004 Tom Wiesner award, given "annually to a Wisconsin-born student-athlete whose loyalty, hard work, spirit and dedication are unselfishly directed to the success of the team." In spring of 2006, he transitioned to cornerback.

"He was pretty versatile in the secondary," Joe Stellmacher confirmed. "He had the ability to play man-to-man. He also had the ability to play center field at safety. It was nice to have a guy with great ball skills and awareness."

"I basically studied every position – strong safety, free safety, the nickel back and the corners. I made myself available to cover any of those positions," Hampton elaborated. "When those opportunities came, whether it was depth issues or just need for that position, I was ready to get out there and go."

That 2007 Capital One Bowl would cap off a Hollywood-like ending to his career, in spite of an at-times difficult 2006 season. He accumulated a plethora of injuries, including broken ribs, fingers and a torn labrum.

With the incumbent Rogers going down in the second quarter of the New Year's Day bowl game, the former walk-on rose to the occasion at free safety. Stellmacher, his teammate for five years, wasn't at all concerned about a drop in production from his peer.

"He was a senior playing his last game, so when he came in, I had no reservations about him whatsoever," Stellmacher asserted. "I knew he'd be up to the task. We certainly were. I remember back to that game and we played some great defense."

With Arkansas driving at the end of the first half, Hampton played far off the line of scrimmage in what's known as a "high safety." He scanned the field hoping to not let anyone get behind him for a possible touchdown, and intercepted a Dick Casey pass at Wisconsin's 5-yard line. The pick halted any scoring opportunity and positive momentum for the Razorbacks heading into the locker room.

Among his five tackles included a perfect read on a dose of

trickery from the Razorbacks – a double-reverse that Hampton thwarted by tackling highly-touted running back Darren McFadden for a one-yard gain in the fourth quarter. It was an exclamation mark on his time as a Badger.

"I was like that most of my career," said Hampton. "Some of my most successful games were games that I wasn't as prepared as I could have been if I was a starter, but I went in and had success in making plays."

****

Like Hampton, Ben Strickland found his niche in the two-deep of Wisconsin's secondary while heavily contributing on special teams. It was that same Capital One Bowl where the reserve found playing time as a cornerback.

According to Stellmacher, there was one point in the game where Strickland was in for starter Allen Langford at cornerback. Three walk-ons were manning and locking down

Zach Hampton (26) and Ben Strickland (3) team up to bring down San Diego State receiver Justin Amaral (85). | AP Photo

the defensive backfield against an SEC team in the biggest game of the year.

"I remember Coach Bielema at the time saying, 'God, my heart was in my throat with you three guys back there,'" Stellmacher said, laughing at the post-game celebration. "He was like, 'How did it ever get to the three of you back there?' But we certainly held our own and I had the utmost confidence with Zach and Ben."

Strickland, a Brookfield native, also had a highlight moment in the second quarter. He burst through the line to block a punt, then recovered the ball to give Wisconsin great field position at the Arkansas 38.

Of course, that wouldn't be *the* punt block and recovery Strickland would be remembered for.

The previous October in the Metrodome, UW fought back from a 10-point Minnesota advantage late in the fourth quarter, when quarterback John Stocco found Williams for a 21-yard touchdown pass. It brought the Badgers back to within a 34-31 game with over two minutes remaining.

After the Gophers recovered the onside kick, the UW defense bucked up and held Minnesota to a three-and-out, forcing their cross-state adversaries to punt. In came punter Justin Kucek, and the Badgers had a choice: either allow Williams to return the kick or attempt a block they had practiced all week for a situation just like this.

"When we were going out there on the field," Strickland said, "you could feel that either we were going to block it or we were going to return it because we had Brandon Williams back there. We had been working on a block all week, basically bringing three up the A-gap."

On the snap, Strickland and Hampton shot up that gap between the long snapper and the guard next to him. The snap wasn't perfect but solid enough to get back to Kucek. He couldn't handle it, however, and the ball floated through his hands onto the turf below. Scrambling, the Gophers' punter picked up the ball and rolled quickly to his right with UW reserve linebacker Jonathan Casillas sprinting towards him with a full head of steam.

Kucek tried to get the kick off quickly.

He didn't.

Casillas blocked the attempt, and a mad dash began between the two walk-ons, Hampton and Strickland, and the athletic linebacker.

"I just remember that the ball was bouncing around there and starting to go to the back of the end zone. Casillas wasn't picking it up himself, so I kind of nudged my way in and dropped on it myself," Strickland said with a huge chuckle.

Strickland's quick thinking would net the go-ahead touchdown and one of the most iconic scores in school history. Television footage showed UW fans jovially screaming and clapping, and an entire sideline of Badgers jumping up and down. Gophers fans stared in shock – dumbfounded a 10-point lead diminished in the final minutes. The play was named the Pontiac Game Changing Performance of the Year for the 2005 season by ESPN.

With the extra point, UW led by four, and after a Gophers fumble on the ensuing kickoff, stole a 38-34 victory to retain Paul Bunyan's Axe.

Strickland played in 51 games from 2004-07 in that special teams and reserve defensive back role. He became a punt blocking guru and a well-respected member of the program, but it was a rocky start for the Brookfield native. After choosing to walk-on and join best friends Steve Johnson and left tackle Joe Thomas in Madison, he had to wait his chance to get into fall camp.

Due to roster attrition, Strickland would get a chance after receiving a phone call from a UW official one evening, telling him to pack his bags and get up to camp the next day. He readied himself for the impromptu, hour-plus long drive to Madison, but his fervor and excitement were quickly dampened as the member of the staff called back later that night.

The one player who initially left would be coming back to the team.

A week later with fall camp already in full swing,

Strickland's name was called again, but this time for good.

Already in Madison but not necessarily in "practice" shape, the strength and conditioning staff pushed him through a rigorous, nauseating, training schedule while the other players were already in full pads and competing in drills.

"At that time, there were a lot of walk-ons that were coming on the team and leaving, so there was a lot of attrition. They wanted to make sure that if you were a walk-on, that you were dedicated. I threw up after every lift and run for four straight days," Strickland said, who pondered if he could make it through a fourth hellacious series of sessions. "I thought I was in pretty good shape until they basically put me through the ringer."

He redshirted that first year while facing the future NFL veteran in Evans numerous times on scout team, something the current Florida Atlantic assistant credits as part of his accelerated development. Coming in at 155 pounds that first season, he added almost 20 pounds to his frame while keeping his agility and quickness.

Like Hampton a year earlier, open tryouts on kickoff coverage gave Strickland a chance to get noticed. He eventually played in all 12 games in that 2004 season. That year was highlighted by his first career punt block against Northwestern – a point of pride that solidified his role in the program.

"When I had made that play, I felt like I was contributing to the team's success," Strickland said, who blocked a third kick in a 17-13 win at home against Iowa in 2007. "I was out there with some great guys that were seniors when I was a freshman, Jim Leonhard and Scott Starks. They were part of the reason I walked on."

He earned a reserve role at cornerback in 2006, which included his first career start and a team-leading six tackles against the Hawkeyes. Later that same season, the coaches bestowed upon him the Badger Power award, presented to the player "that consistently performs at a high level in all aspects of the strength and conditioning program."

He earned much-deserved accolades during his time at Wisconsin: Award recipient, Academic All-Big Ten honoree, dependable defensive back, and special teams ace.

There would be one more role he'd earn while a player for the Wisconsin Badgers, however – captain.

To those who've known the 5-foot-9 athlete, the future coach personified the Wisconsin way. He earned his peers' respect on and off the field. He pushed other players to maximize their abilities to the fullest.

In 2007, three of the five captains would be walk-ons, as DeBauche, Swan and Strickland were elected to lead the team.

"He's just a very competitive, serious, hard-working guy that just embodied leadership," Thomas said, who's known Strickland since elementary school. "He's a coach right now, and that's what he loves doing, and he's always liked being the role model, a mentor. He's done it his whole life. He had high school and middle school kids he was mentoring when he was in college, so that's always been an important part of his life. I kind of expected him to be a leader on that Badger team once he became an upperclassman."

"I was competitive," Strickland said honestly, "so even though some guys may have been bigger, faster, stronger, I always trained to not lose and to compete. I think, and hope, that's why people recognized me as a leader. I didn't really need to say much; I didn't feel that was necessarily my place. When something had to be said, I had no problem saying it, but I felt it was more important to lead by example.

"Being named captain was something I was surprised by. It was very humbling knowing I had that respect from my teammates. So for me it was another thing that motivated me to give it my best and be who I was, work hard, and do all the things that got me to that point."

With the leadership and mentorship exhibited during his playing days, it was only a natural progression Strickland would find a home in the coaching game. He returned to Wisconsin as a graduate assistant and was later elevated to defensive backs and cornerbacks coach from 2009-14.

Heading into 2016, he enters his second season molding defensive backs as part of FAU's football staff.

CHAPTER NINE

The Unheralded and Outcast: The Specialists

Ben Strickland and Steve Johnson grew up together as neighbors in the Milwaukee suburb of Brookfield. When Strickland's family had to work during sports tournaments, Johnson's family would take him in like another son. Both players came to Wisconsin as walk-ons, both made their marks on special teams, and both earned scholarships heading into their redshirt sophomore seasons in 2005.

Years later, they would even be each other's best man in their respective weddings.

That history is what made Strickland's decision to give up his scholarship, so his best friend could keep his, that much easier for the 2007 season.

"They always took care of me," Strickland said about their bond, "never asked me for anything, never did anything to make me feel like I was imposing. I had only three credits left. Three credits weren't that expensive so I felt like I could handle that on my own and thought I would have some free time to work and make money.

"I didn't think it was that big of a deal. Steve had a full year left, and with his family, and for how much they did for me and how close we were, it was an easy decision. For walkons your scholarship was one year, I guess that was the scenario for all scholarships at the time, but for the walk-ons, it was really year-to-year."

In a meeting before the 2007 season, Johnson found out that he would have his scholarship pulled. The former Greater Metro Conference Offensive Lineman of the Year walked on as a linebacker then won the starting long snapper job in 2005, but he knew that the scholarship could be snatched away at any moment.

When he found out he would have to pay his way for his final year it was a punch to the gut. He felt, however, the coaching staff had every right to make the best decision for Wisconsin.

"I played eight plays a game, so who am I to say that it's unfair?" Johnson acknowledged, his tone sincere but direct. "In my opinion it was fair. At the same time, there's that same type of emotional swing you have when you're put on scholarship – you're absolutely elated. When they take it away, you're crushed."

Though understanding, Johnson wasn't thrilled with the news. With the prospects of his best friend having to pay for room and board yet again, Strickland made a very "simple" call. It was one he wanted to keep private, and not communicate to the public.

Though gracious and appreciative of his friend's generous offer, the long snapper wasn't happy with Strickland just giving up his free ride. He felt his childhood buddy deserved keeping his scholarship.

"He was a captain, a leadership guy. He was the heart," Johnson glowed about Strickland. "He deserved it even though he didn't have a 'starting position.' We both started on special teams. You're happy when he tells you, but you feel like he deserves it more than you. He felt differently on it. At the same time, I don't know if I was that surprised. 'Strick' puts everyone before himself."

"It was not surprising at all to me," Joe Thomas said of the gesture. "(Strickland's) just that type of wonderful person. He really cares about people and never his own accolades, and he never thinks about himself first."

Early on, long snappers weren't necessarily known for

being "specialists," as many back-up position players would contribute to their respective teams in this role. Over time, it became more defined and appreciated.

The specialists normally don't stay for all of the allotted practice time. Different from the rest of the position groups, their exact skill set allows them the luxury of not participating in blocking and tackling drills.

"They would do their warm-ups, and the special teams segment, but then they would go inside for the next two hours before the end of practice," Thomas laughed. "Then they would come out with JD (former strength and conditioning coach John Dettman) and the strength staff and take a knee on the sidelines like they had been there the whole time.

"To top it off, they would always be the first ones in line at training table, acting like they were working hard, eating all of our food, drinking all of our water, breathing all of our air!"

The last statement from Thomas is facetious, of course, and one made with a jovial chuckle that couldn't hide his true feelings.

The Cleveland Browns All-Pro tackle should know a thing or two about this particular group of players. Aside from being best friends with Johnson and Strickland, he also befriended kicker Taylor Mehlhaff and punters Paul Standring and DeBauche. In fact, all of them stood up in Standring's wedding.

The specialists sometimes receive the short end of the stick when it comes to acknowledgment from the fans, as well as teammates.

As was the case with Schnetzky, the head coach may not remember your name. At Wisconsin, some walk-on specialists had to push certain buttons to even get noticed, but there are those that have flourished, kicking their way into the record books. Others have been endearing members of their respective teams with their unique personalities or their witty charm.

All forged a bond as a "team within a team" to help propel

themselves and the Badgers to victories, championships, and good ole-fashioned laughs.

They may have disappeared at times, but they were also the ones out early before the team's scheduled practices, sometimes a half-hour to an hour prior working on their snapping, kicking and punting with the entire field at their disposal. Though they're not technically partaking in team activities, their contributions to the game don't need to be worn down over several two-plus hour practices each week.

"It's sort of like a pitcher. You can't get better at pitching if you pitch every day," DeBauche explained. "There has to be some rest, there has to be other exercises. You have to work on other things that you're doing."

The down time was mostly spent together relaxing or playing games. Matt Davenport pointed out that he and his specialist crew would watch "Oprah" to pass the time. Many, like kicker Mike Allen, made ping pong their go-to game. Andrew Endicott and Co. now enjoy a table in the players' lounge inside Camp Randall Stadium.

Allen also remembers playing a game called "garbage can," where they would set an object at the end of the field and see which player could get the ball in first. There was also "Polf," reminiscent to golf, where they would have to switch off throwing and punting to get a ball in a garbage can in the least amount of strokes.

The current crop of specialists plays "Ultimate Specialist," in which the competitors have to long snap, punt and kick their way to victory either through recording the longest distance or by hitting a designated target.

"There's the time where we've done our kicking, punting and snapping. We've worked out, we're at the point where we can't do any more to really make ourselves better. A lot of what we did sounds like we goofed off a lot. We had a lot of fun, but we earned our fun," DeBauche said. "We worked harder than any other specialists group in the conference, maybe in the country."

****

Like their teammates, specialists compete for playing time. Sometimes the stakes would grow larger for those that were walk-ons, as a potential scholarship was on the line.

Vitaly Pisetsky and Matt Davenport were both recruited in the last half of John Hall's Wisconsin career.

Davenport came from Orange County, Calif., a son of a pastor who played eight-man football at Capital Valley Christian and graduated from a class of only 35. He went to Saddleback College and excelled in both baseball and football. He credits a gentleman by the name of Jack Murray for his chance to play at Wisconsin. Murray told assistant Kevin Cosgrove about the kicker when the coaching staff was looking at another standout at the community college named David Cruickshank.

Though the Wisconsin assistant is mentioned as his lead recruiter, Davenport never spoke with him or other coaches during his courtship to UW, and never took an official visit to Madison. It was a gut-check call on his part, and he took the walk-on opportunity when it was presented.

Technically, Pisetsky was offered a scholarship out of high school, but was ruled ineligible as an NCAA non-qualifier for his first season due to missing one year of English after emigrating from Russia in the tenth grade (NCAA regulations stated four years were needed) despite placing in the 97th percentile in the university's English placement exam.

Pisetsky came to Wisconsin a Blue Chip All-American and two-time all-state selection from Kennedy High School. Unlike Davenport, the former Russian National soccer team member came from a school of several thousand.

Though both came in during Hall's senior year, Davenport would see the field in limited time, making all three extra points he attempted. Pisetsky sat out that initial freshman year but still attended school.

The stage was set for the two to face off starting in the spring of 1997.

What added to the intrigue of the battle was the fact they were also roommates.

Moses Sankey, a former walk-on wide receiver, ate dinner with Davenport after the first spring practice of the season. The teammate asked the 5-foot-7, 160-pound Californian about the first day of competition.

"I said, 'Oh, I did pretty well, I made three out of four field goals. He literally punched me in the chest, grabbed my collar, and said, 'You don't miss again!'" Davenport laughed. "I snapped into focus, and I gotta thank Moses for that. Maybe I was just scared of him. I didn't miss the entire rest of the spring."

The competition would go into fall camp. Davenport was solid within his range, while Vitaly had the leg strength that was Hall-esque in nature. In the end, the accuracy of the West Coast kid won out for the placekicking duties for field goals and extra points, though Pisetsky still found himself contributing on the team.

"The hardest thing was probably losing the place kicking job to Matt in '97, because that messed with my confidence a bit," Pisetsky confessed. "I had the kickoff job locked up, but

was kicking field goals at about 70-75 percent in camp, which for a freshman kicker isn't bad at all.

Matt Davenport (28) earned the nickname "Money" with plenty of clutch kicks while at UW. | Wisconsin State Journal

Matt was kicking at 90 percent. He proved to be mentally tougher for those years.

"We were roommates, we supported each other, and we were really good friends – but it was a real competition. I remember when he made those kicks back-to-back against Indiana and Northwestern. That's when I knew the job was basically gone."

Confidence is a must-have for a placekicker. They perform in front of tens of thousands of screaming fans with the game on the line. A kick could clinch an undefeated season, a critical road win, or the chance to go to a bowl game.

For Davenport, whose 43-yarder against Indiana came on his parents' 25th wedding anniversary, he tried to understand the importance of the moment. Feeling a part of the team, he had guys come up to him and say they were behind him whether he made it or missed it, but he didn't want to let them down. Then again, he realized it's just one kick. It was a simple boot of the ball that many wanted to see go through those uprights to lift the team to win, but it was just like any other he's attempted.

"I think I'm pretty mentally tough, but there's nothing to prepare you to kick in front of 85,000 people and feeling that sort of pressure," Davenport stated. "I tried to overcome that by working as hard as I could and having no regrets. I didn't want to think, 'Oh, I wish I would have worked harder.'"

With his accuracy and kicking display during spring and summer camps, Davenport was well respected by his teammates. He even earned a nickname that he accidentally gave himself.

After practice, a reporter asked him what his range was. The confident placekicker responded that he was pretty much "money" from 45 yards in. He immediately regretted those words.

Confiding in some of the offensive linemen group, which included walk-ons Tauscher and Eck, he told them what happened during the interview. According to Davenport, they shrugged it off, noting it wouldn't become a big deal.

Well, it kind of did.

According to Davenport, they would post the articles of the team in the seminary hall during fall camp. A couple of days later, he remembered getting ready for practice when special teams coach Jay Hayes walked up.

"What's up 'Money!" Davenport remembered Hayes saying.

The razzing and torment weren't over. Fellow assistant John Palermo then came over to the startled junior, challenging him to put his 'money' where his mouth was. Confident in his abilities, his next three kicks would cement a moniker that stuck for the rest of his career. He still holds the single-season school record for field goal percentage (90.5 in 1998).

"They lined up three field goals from 45 yards for Vitaly and I. If you've ever hit a perfect drive in golf, it was that type of moment. I just crushed these right down the middle – the best kicks I ever had in my whole life," said Davenport, who also still holds the school-record for career field goal percentage (33-of-38, or 86.8 percent). "After that, all the guys just started calling me 'Money.'"

"It was such a defining moment for me. It was just a comment, but it really forced me to kind of own it."

****

Davenport won two games with his leg in 1997, but never in a bowl game setting. Fast forward five years, and Mike Allen drilled a 37-yard attempt to lift the Badgers to a 31-28 victory over Colorado in the 2002 Valero Alamo Bowl.

After a fourth-quarter comeback sent the game to overtime, UW's defense held the Buffaloes' offense without a touchdown. Kicker Pat Brougham missed a 45-yard attempt that sailed wide right, giving the Badgers a chance.

With Wisconsin's offense advancing the ball to the 20-yard line, it was Allen's turn to play hero. From the hold of backup quarterback Matt Schabert, Allen went through a kicking motion he's done thousands of times before, and put

Kicker Mike Allen (97) celebrates his 37-yard field goal lifting the Badgers to a 31-28 overtime victory over Colorado in the 2002 Valero Alamo Bowl. | AP Photo

it through the uprights. Television replays showed the kicker looking at the sideline and immediately raising both arms in celebration.

"I don't even remember that kick," Allen admitted. "I remember before and afterwards. From the time I walked on that field, to the time I walked off, it's a blank memory."

Despite the memory lapse, the 6-foot-2, 182-pound kicker best remembers his mindset from a conversation he had with a teammate. Cornerback Scott Starks once told him defensive backs can't worry about the play before because that has no impact on the upcoming play. It would be a lesson learned early on for Allen.

The year prior, he won the placekicking job as a true freshman but ultimately lost it to fellow walk-on Mark Neuser a third of the way through the season. Through the first four games, the Prescott, Wis. native went 6-of-9 on attempts, including a 50-yard boot against Fresno State. Unfortunately, two missed field goals plus a missed extra point in Wisconsin's 18-6 win at Penn State sealed his fate.

Allen earned the job back the following year over junior college All-American Scott Campbell and Adam Espinoza. He instantly delivered, kicking what would be the game-winning, 34-yard field goal in Leonhard's coming out party against Fresno State. That season he converted 12-of-19 attempts, with greater success from inside 40 yards (8-of-10).

"Coach Alvarez would stress this a lot: 'We're on a business trip, whether it's an away game or a home game, we're here to do business and take care of business.' I took that to heart," noted Allen, who ranks fifth all-time in school history in field goals made (41) and sixth in extra points (97).

"Every time we were on a trip, or in a game, or in practice, I was there to do my job and that's how I conducted myself. Some days I succeeded. Other days I failed miserably. The next day was a new day. Yesterday doesn't matter, it's what I'm doing today that counts."

****

The pressure may be high at times, but the specialists at Wisconsin know how to unwind. Two punters in particular, DeBauche and Standring, brought out the best in each other on and off the field. They came in the same year as Strickland and Johnson in 2003, but were competing for the starting punter job alongside incumbent and fellow walk-on R.J. Morse. Both earned honorable mention all-state honors – Standring played at St. Rita in the Chicagoland area, while DeBauche played for Bay Port High School up in Green Bay.

"I think our relationship was really kind of built upon playing catch. We'd sit on the sideline during practice and just toss the ball back and forth and 'BS' about everything but football," DeBauche joked. "Really talking about anything other than what our job was, which was punting."

Being walk-ons they didn't have access to the training table the scholarship players would get to eat at. They had a choice of consuming the Easy Mac macaroni or saltines sitting in their dorms or create their own set of "scavenger hunts" to feed themselves.

"We'd go on the girls' floors in Ogg and ask for whatever we were hungry for, and for their phone number because you got bonus points for those," Standring explained in greater detail.

"Paul was a little more shameless than I was," DeBauche laughed. "I think he was in it to get the food, where maybe when we created those fake scavenger hunts, I might have been motivated to ultimately get the girls' phone numbers."

They would have their fun, but that was just who they were. Especially Standring, who had a vibrant and outgoing personality.

"He was one of the funniest guys you've ever talked to," BadgerBlitz.com's Jon McNamara acknowledged. "He used to ride around campus on an old, two-seater bike. A lot of guys had mopeds, but he would just ride around on this tandem bike. Sometimes he'd be by himself, sometimes he'd have a girl on back. He definitely had a personality of a happy-go-lucky guy."

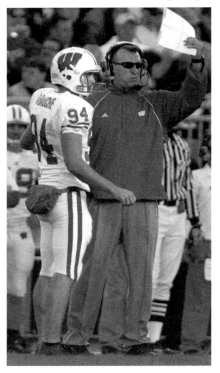

Ken Debauche with former coach Brett Bielema. Since 1990 Debauche is the only punter or kicker to be named a UW captain. | AP Photo

As noted earlier, the specialists knew how to have a good time.

Once, a group of six had the opportunity to bust out the golf clubs during the middle of two-a-day practices. The specialists only had to participate in the morning workout so Standring, DeBauche, Johnson, Mehlhaff, and reserves Dave Peck and Matt Fischer spent a wonderful afternoon golfing at Vitense Golfland on the west side of Madison.

"On the ninth hole at Vitense, which is about 140 yards long, Matt Fischer pulled out his nine iron, and hit a nice shot straight at the pin," DeBauche recalled with amazing clarity. "It landed on the front half of the green and rolled right up for a hole-in-one."

Pandemonium ensued.

"We all went crazy," Debauche remembered. "It was awesome. To this day, it was the only hole-in-one that I've witnessed. We got back to the locker room and wanted to share our excitement so we posted it up on the board. I don't think anybody was too excited that we were golfing while they were watching film and doing football stuff."

"Guys were like, 'Are you serious? You went golfing during the second practice?' Johnson recollected. "We said, 'Yeah, man. It was great!' They said, 'Screw you guys.'"

"But hey, we're the specialists. We came. We did our work. We accomplished everything we needed to accomplish for that day. All the coaches were satisfied with what we did. If we have absolutely nothing to do at practice, we could stand around and watch, or we could golf."

For all the shenanigans they found themselves in, a few walk-on specialists earned accolades for their kicking ability.

Davenport was a two-time first-team All-Big Ten selection and in contention for the Lou Groza award, given to college football's best placekicker. DeBauche was elected first-team all-conference for his efforts in 2005 when he led the Big Ten in yards per punt (44.8), still the single-season school record. That year, *Sports Illustrated* named him to their second-team All-American squad.

The Green Bay native would earn even higher praise from

his teammates. Since 1990, he is the only punter or kicker to be named a captain.

"Man, it was an honor, and something I am still honored by for a number of reasons," DeBauche noted. "One is that I was a walk-on. Somebody that was sort of an outsider looking in, whether it was on the practice field or hoping that I could be a starter someday, or standing outside the training table and seeing all the scholarship guys getting their free meal, hoping I can be in there with them someday.

"There's the walk-on part of it, but also earning my spot on the field, earning my spot amongst my teammates as somebody that's a leader. As a specialist, I'm in for 10 plays a game. That's not a lot of plays where I can really show my leadership on the field."

He averaged 41.6 yards per punt in his final year at UW, good for third in the conference, and would ultimately finish second in school history (42.5). That season, he would also complete his only pass in his career as well to his partner-in-crime, Standring.

Standring comes from a lineage of college football players. His father played at Notre Dame, while two of his uncles played at Miami and Illinois. His brother, J.J., punted at Northwestern. After losing out on the punting duties to Morse and DeBauche, he continued on the team without a scholarship.

In 2007 as a fifth-year senior, Standring would finally get his opportunity to play consistently. In 12 games, he registered 11 tackles, and his claim to fame would be the 31-yard reception against future NFL draft pick Marcus Freeman.

Heading into UW's match-up against No. 1 Ohio State in the Horseshoe, Bielema would give the go ahead for a special teams surprise in Columbus.

The fake punt was supposed to work in the following way:

Long-snapper Steve Johnson would snap the ball back to DeBauche, who would then roll and look to the right trying to fool the defense before passing back to a wide-open receiver on the left side.

According to DeBauche, Wisconsin had run a similar play in 2006. The play worked out perfectly in the fourth quarter of what would turn out to be a 24-3 Wisconsin win. Unfortunately, Jonathan Casillas, who was the intended receiver, dropped the pass.

While planning out the fake punt, DeBauche half-jokingly recommended Standring in that spot of the receiver. With the "chemistry" the two developed throwing the ball thousands of times together on the sideline, the team decided to go with him.

The excitement seeped through Standring's pores, almost to a fault.

"Leading up to that game, knowing that there was a very high likelihood that we were going to be running that play, I remember talking with Paul the night before. He had been talking with friends and telling them, 'You gotta watch the game because we're going to run this fake punt!' I said, 'Paul, you can't be telling people that we're going to run a fake.'"

"He did everything short of posting it on Facebook."

The UW coaching staff would deploy the fake early in the game. With the Buckeyes already leading 7-0 after their opening drive, the Badgers faced a 4th-and-12 from their own 47-yard line. The 6-foot-1, 213-pound Standring would get his chance to shine. Some improvisation would be needed, however, as Freeman didn't bite on the fake. He kept his assignment and stayed on him.

"On film, the moment the ball was snapped (Freeman) would usually turn and sprint 15-20 yards towards the punt returner to identify where the ball was being punted, and then start working his way up the field to block for the punt returner," said Standring. "The moment the ball was snapped, I fake blocked for a second or two. For some crazy reason, as I ran out for what should have been a short pass, Freeman started following me. We did not prepare for that, so I just kept running down the field hoping Kenny would still throw me the rock."

"I look to the left, and there's a linebacker on Paul, and he just takes off," DeBauche vividly recalled. "I don't think I had any other thought than completing the pass. I didn't know if I waited for Paul to get a step, but I just launched it. I dropped a dime in there right on the money. Paul made a beautiful catch on the sideline, then fell into the Ohio State punting and kicking net."

Wisconsin would take that momentum and convert a field goal to make it a 7-3 game. Though UW took a 17-10 lead on the road midway through the third quarter, Ohio State would score 28 unanswered points in a 38-17 victory. Though the loss would push them to 3-3 in conference play, the best friends would have this memory for years to come despite the hiccups in the initial game plan.

"Ben (Strickland) always makes fun of me for screaming 'YEAH!' after the catch, but I didn't know what to do or say," Standring declared with a laugh. "The place was just silent, and I felt like everything was in slow motion after the catch. I was wondering why people weren't cheering then remembered we were in Columbus and realized, '100,000 people hate me right now.'"

"I might have blacked out for a second," DeBauche said, "but I remember being really excited, really pumped that he caught the ball. I could see from where I threw it that he caught it. I just remember running down the field, trying to get down there to give Paul a high-five or a hug."

"Kenny was giving fist pump after fist pump thinking he was Brett Favre or something," Standring recalled. "The thing is, Kenny and I had probably forty different handshakes we made up together, and all we ended up doing was a high-five – and we missed. That would have been the perfect time to bust out one of the fantastic handshakes we had, but we totally blew it."

The bond between DeBauche and Standring isn't uncommon in the football world, but is pretty much the norm in the world of specialists. Specialists start out as competitors. They vie for limited playing time, spending countless hours together working on their craft. Friendships form, some become roommates, and some even wind up being groomsmen in each other's weddings.

There's also a fraternal aspect that transcends a single football program.

"We understand each other better than the other guys do," said Endicott, who has friends that kick at Texas A&M, Cincinnati and South Carolina. "The other guys see us just kicking or punting some balls and think anyone can do that. They don't see us coming in here and trying to get better every day. Someone sees 'Rafa' (Wisconsin placekicker Rafael Gaglianone) miss a field goal or I hit a bad kickoff. They say, 'How did you miss that?' For us, we understand the ins and outs, the little things."

The position groups may not understand them, at least not completely. For all the eclectic tendencies and attitudes, they remain key members of the football program. That especially holds true at Wisconsin, where many have walked on and flourished.

"If I ever coach, I want my specialists loose," former UW tight end Owen Daniels said. "Because if you really think about what they have to do, it's so specialized, and they're under a lot of pressure. During a field goal or a punting situation, all that stuff needs to be pin point to have a chance to be successful. If you're loose and not uptight, you're better off."

CHAPTER TEN

The Time to Shine

Josh Hunt wasn't supposed to be the starting punt returner in the 2000 season opener against Western Michigan. Incumbent Nick Davis was a dynamic playmaker and was slated to continue handling the duties heading into a year where UW's momentum was at an all-time high after back-to-back Rose Bowl championships.

That momentum was halted when suspensions from the Shoe Box affair came down mere hours before the Badgers faced the Broncos. The university conducted an internal investigation, based on reports from the *Wisconsin State Journal*, starting in July 2000. UW student-athletes accepted discounts and lines of credit from The Shoe Box, a store about 25 miles northwest of Madison.

Heading into the 2000 opener against Western Michigan, 26 members of the football team were suspended between one and three games to start the year. Their penalties would be served within the first four contests of the season. Eleven UW players wouldn't be allowed to suit up against the Broncos. Hunt remembers Alvarez explaining the sanctions to the players a couple of hours before the game.

Assistant coach Kevin Cosgrove approached Hunt and explained Davis would have to sit. Hunt's only claim to fame to that point had been his scout team offensive player of the week honors against Boise State in 1997. This night in Camp Randall Stadium, however, he would be a critical contributor.

"Coach Alvarez came to me and said, 'Are you good with

this? Can you handle this?'" Hunt recollected. "I said, 'Yeah, I definitely can.'

"There was no doubt in my mind I was ready."

Emotions of excitement and nervousness flooded the back-up returner. Hunt's parents were coming to the game from their hometown, Thiensville, just outside of Mequon. They had no idea of their son's new role until they heard about the impromptu suspensions on the radio.

Hunt had waited years for this opportunity. A second-team all-state selection by the *Milwaukee Journal Sentinel* out of Homestead High School, he had primarily seen work as a scout team wide receiver for Wisconsin. He did have special teams experience in his prep years, averaging over 18 yards per return with two touchdowns during his senior year.

According to Hunt, the opportunity to walk-on came about when Brian White, UW's offensive coordinator at the time, was at a Homestead game where Hunt scored on a punt return. Hunt considered Dartmouth and South Dakota, and also took an official visit to Northern Michigan. In the end, he joined his high school teammate, Scott Williams, and made the decision to come to Madison.

Playing primarily on scout team and being buried on the depth chart, there were moments of doubt. He broke his collarbone and thought about quitting altogether, especially with Williams leaving the program. He contemplated reaching back out to Dartmouth but never did. There was a discussion with Unertl, who transferred from Division III up to the Division I ranks, about the pros and cons associated with moving down competition levels.

"We talked in depth about it," Unertl said. "Being from the state, getting a degree from the University of Wisconsin and the network of alumni, and comparing that to going to a school like La Crosse or Whitewater just to play football."

Those talks refocused Hunt as to why he came to Wisconsin in the first place – which for him meant a complete commitment to the program.

"From that point on, I knew I was going to stick with it

Josh Hunt (20) takes a punt return 89-yards for a touchdown versus Western Michigan in 2000. | Wisconsin State Journal

and try to get on the field," Hunt said.

On that hazy Thursday evening at Camp Randall Stadium with temperatures around 90 degrees, he would finally have the opportunity to field a ball late in the first quarter. The Badgers' defense forced the Broncos to punt for the first of six times. Hunt was able to field the 40-yard boot, but lost a yard on the return.

Hunt also had to jump through another hoop that evening. A wide receiver by position, he wore No. 23. B.J. Tucker, a defensive back, also wore the same number. Both Hunt and Tucker were now on the field during punt returns. The refs let Wisconsin know, and Hunt would have to change out of his jersey. The UW staff scurried and found a new jersey – No. 20 – but it wouldn't have his name on the back for the first half.

Wisconsin and Western Michigan's offensive drives each stalled until late in the second quarter with the Badgers still clinging to a field goal advantage.

Hunt backtracked to UW's own 11-yard line to catch the

Broncos punt. He turned up field and, after breaking a tackle and slipping past a couple defenders, received a block from Lee Evans that thwarted any Broncos attempt at catching him.

It was off to the races for the 5-foot-9, 180-pound returner.

"I made a cut around Lee and then the next thing I know, all I saw was 50 yards to the end zone," Hunt recalled. "My biggest fear at that moment was, I know there are fast guys out here and if they catch me from behind – I'm going to be so mad."

Eighty-nine yards later, Hunt crossed the goal line that would give UW a 10-0 lead, and ultimately were the deciding points in Wisconsin's 19-7 win. The collarbone injury, the moments of wavering if he should continue playing at UW, were all left behind as he raced down the field for the second longest punt return in school history.

"When I hit the end zone, I heard the crowd, turned around, and (tight end) Mark Anelli grabbed the front of my shoulder pads and hoisted me up," Hunt remembered fondly.

"Right at that moment, the four years, all the developmental workouts, any doubts that I ever had were wiped away, just for that one moment. It was pretty spectacular."

It's something his friend, who helped convince Hunt to stick with it, will never forget.

"When something like that happens for a guy like Josh, who started out in a very similar way to me, you're just ecstatic for him," Unertl said, recalling the shivers he had watching his teammate extend the Badgers' lead. "Sometimes all it takes is that opportunity, right?

A scandal disrupted a run for a third consecutive conference title and higher aspirations, but there were rays of sunshine through the cloudy days set over the Wisconsin program during the 2000 season.

"Part of the beauty of sports is when something like this happens, it creates an opportunity for someone else, and that was Josh Hunt's night," Badgers play-by-play man Matt Lepay recalled. "People will remember that name. They may not remember who they played that night. They have long forgotten that Western Michigan was the opponent, but they will remember that some kid named Josh Hunt had the game of his life."

****

Suspensions and a scandal allowed Hunt to finally see the field and make an impact during that 2000 season. Injuries hampered linebacker Ben Ruechel's ability to produce on the field early on in his career, but he rebounded to contribute on special teams and in a reserve role on defense.

Like Hunt, he had waited the majority of his career to contribute. It wasn't the plan for the honorable mention all-state selection from Oconto, Wis.

While Hunt had the broken collarbone, Ruechel dealt with knee issues that kept him sidelined for good parts of 2012 and 2013. On his official biography page on UWBadgers.com, he redshirted his first year on the team in 2010. The following three seasons the same three words were repeated line after line, year after year: Did. Not. Play.

He suffered a torn ACL in his right knee the first padded practice of the 2012 season, sidelining him for an entire year in which he was expected to contribute on special teams. He rebounded, but with Bielema bolting to Fayetteville, Ruechel (pronounced REEK-ull) not only had to adjust to Gary Andersen's 3-4 defense, but also fight through lingering issues with a cartilage tear in his left knee. A surgery in October 2013 halted another chance to break through.

There were, however, other meaningful ways to assist the team while not on the field, including helping keep teammates prepared for each week's game plan.

"I just feel there are two roles that you don't really see Sunday after the game in the box scores, but they're important to the team. I was fortunate that I could be a part of that and contribute to the success, and we had pretty good years over my career," said Ruechel.

Finally, his health and opportunities would allow him to

break through in 2014, playing in all 14 games. Finally, he had the chance to see action on special teams – playing on the punt return, kickoff return and kickoff teams. With inside linebackers Chris Borland and Conor O'Neill gone, he had a legitimate shot to contribute on defense.

Finally.

"People on the outside have no idea the work you have to put in for a walk-on," teammate Marcus Trotter pointed out. "Ruechel had to work his tail off for five years just to get a chance to play on special teams."

"Wisconsin's coaches are really good about giving you a shot on special teams, but when your number's called, you got to perform," Ruechel said. "Fortunately for me, I was able to perform well in practice. I had a good fall camp defensively and on special teams."

On October 11, 2014, the Badgers hosted the Illini at Camp Randall Stadium but without Trotter due to a groin injury. Leon Jacobs took Trotter's place that afternoon, but during the game, starter Derek Landisch suffered a left elbow injury, leaving him out of the contest temporarily.

Two senior leaders of the defense were out of the game. Enter Ruechel.

The Illini offense, trying to answer a Melvin Gordon six-yard touchdown run, faced a 3rd-and-6 from its own 34. Ruechel recalled the Badgers' defense had trouble getting their opponents' offense into third down situations. It was time to turn up the pressure.

"Defensive coordinator Dave Aranda called the blitz that he wanted, and we got the protection scheme that we had anticipated, and it opened up nicely in the middle," Ruechel said.

Ruechel blew past Illinois center Joe Spencer and sacked quarterback Peter O'Toole. The resulting eight-yard loss would force Illinois to punt. Celebrations ensued on the sideline.

"You think my head would be spinning that first time on the field, but I had been practicing against one of the best offensive lines in the nation for five years," Ruechel said. "It was a good feeling. I think I was more proud of the fact that I was able to help my team than get my first sack or get my first significant time on the field."

That sack was one of six on the afternoon in UW's 38-28 victory. It would be Ruechel's only tackle of the afternoon, one of seven on the season.

His path to college football took him to the only in-state Division I program after turning down opportunities from Division II schools. Setbacks derailed earlier attempts to play between the hashes, but there are no regrets or second guesses on Ruechel's part.

"If the setbacks didn't happen, maybe my career could have gone in a different direction, but you gotta do the best with the hand you're dealt," Ruechel admitted, who was awarded a scholarship before his senior season. "You can't really do anything about the things you can't control. I feel satisfied with my career."

"(Ruechel) never complained at all. Never worried about it," Trotter said, "and I've always admired him for it."

****

Hunt's punt return and Ruechel's sack each served as a momentum changing play during a key moment of each game.

Nate Tice's 17-yard touchdown run against Indiana in 2010, however, was much different. It didn't seal a victory or begin a year-plus reign for Tice as starting quarterback in Paul Chryst's pro-style offense.

The play call the fourth-year junior scored on wasn't designed to do anything more than move the chains and take time off the clock late in the fourth quarter.

It ended up being *the* play in the third stringer's legacy.

"That might have been the most excitement of the season when he scored that touchdown," offensive guard Kevin Zeitler recalled. "If there was ever a guy that you weren't sure he'd ever get in the game, it was Nate."

It was a long journey to see the field for Tice. Four years

earlier, he originally committed to Central Florida as a first-team all-conference and all-state honorable mention quarterback out of Edina, Minn. Ranked a two-star commit and the second best quarterback in the state by Rivals.com, he admitted he verbally pledged to the Golden Knights too early after receiving an offer from then-head coach George O'Leary.

There was a connection to Central Florida, as O'Leary coached Nate's dad, Mike, in high school. Many football fans know the elder Tice as the head coach of the Minnesota Vikings from 2001-05 and a long-time NFL assistant.

O'Leary had served as Tice's assistant from 2002-2003 with the Vikings before moving on to the UCF job in 2004. At the time, Nate wanted the recruiting process to be over, so he committed in September 2006.

Tice realized his time in the Orlando area wouldn't last and sought to transfer. He visited FCS schools, but he wanted to go to a bigger school and a bigger program, even if it meant he would have to walk-on. He looked at and inquired about Iowa and Wisconsin. According to "Ticer," his nickname from former teammates, the Hawkeyes would have a spot on their team for him, but Badgers assistant coach Randall McCray extended an invitation to come out for an official visit during spring football.

"After being at UCF and realizing what I did and did not like, I went to Wisconsin. I was like, 'Alright, they practice tough but it's a good way of tough. It's not just guys yelling at you – it's good coaching,'" Tice said. "I'll be walking on as a fifth or sixth string quarterback, but Coach Chryst treats everyone exactly the same."

He decided to walk-on at Wisconsin but had to sit out the 2009 season. One of the new kids in the program, his locker sat right next to one of Wisconsin's emerging offensive stars, a heralded running back named John Clay.

"I'm sitting next to him, and he's big time. He's never going to talk with me," Tice thought. "And John asks, 'Hey, what's your name?'"

Clay knew Tice was from Minnesota. They exchanged

introductions and pleasantries. Then in a surprising move, Clay gave him his number and asked him what he was up to – a microcosm of the warm relationships and mentality Wisconsin players share between each other, whether walk-on or scholarship player.

"He said 'alright, call me, let's go hang out,' … that's just how Wisconsin was," Tice said. "Everybody got along, no one was too big for the team, and for John Clay in week one – I'm just a walk-on quarterback – for him to act like that, I knew I made the right choice."

The transfer quarterback saw Scott Tolzien emerge as the starter to lead the UW offense after what he described as one

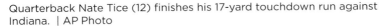

Quarterback Nate Tice (12) finishes his 17-yard touchdown run against Indiana. | AP Photo

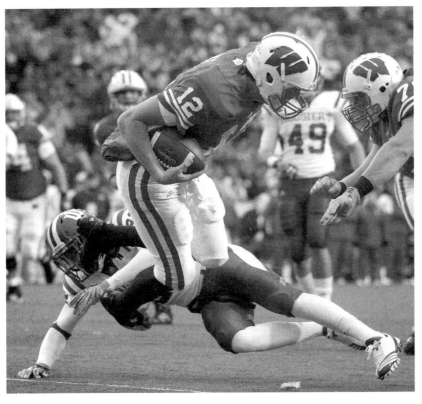

of the best summer camps he's ever seen a quarterback have.

Heading into the spring of 2010, Tice competed with the incumbent Tolzien, a promising quarterback in Curt Phillips, and Jon Budmayr for reps at quarterback. Unfortunately, Phillips tore the ACL in his right knee during spring practices, leaving Tice in the position of being third on the depth chart.

The opportunity would allow him to receive some more reps and responsibility, and he ended up being one of the signal callers from the sidelines, signaling in plays from the coach to the quarterbacks. Tice contends it was the most coaching he's ever had, working side-by-side with Chryst for an hour at a time during practices, but there was an added bonus when game time came around – Tice's mug was shown when the television shots cut to the coaching staff on the sideline.

"It was a running joke, 'Nate Tice doesn't get any reps but he's getting more face time (on television) than anybody,'" he recalled with a chuckle.

The future NFL scouting assistant got his moment to shine on the field with the Badgers up 76-20 against the Hoosiers and 4:59 remaining.

Chryst, with his dry sense of humor, foreshadowed Tice's entrance into the game, albeit jokingly at first.

"So he's sitting there, and at the end of the third quarter, he goes, 'Hey Nate, you loose?'"

"I go, 'What?!?!'" Tice recalled with a laugh.

"'Get ready to run, I'm going to call Lonesome.'"

Tice laughed, but with less than five minutes left in regulation, there he was, about to lead UW starting at its own 32-yard line. Wisconsin's offense mostly consisted of third-team players at that point in the blowout.

Despite the back-ups playing, UW moved the ball efficiently. Running back James White pushed the ball into Hoosiers territory again with a 44-yard scamper to the Indiana 23. Two runs by Kyle Zuleger, then still a running back, set up a 3rd-and-4 from the 17. In a game against

Austin Peay earlier in the year, Tice came in and just handed off to the backs. Four plays into game action on that Saturday, he did just the same. On the next play, Chryst would call his number.

"Nate was our last quarterback on the roster that hadn't gone in yet, and I think he'd be the first to tell you that he would not believe that he could outrun an entire defense," Bielema said. "We called a bootleg play just to kind of see if we could move the chains and get a first down without throwing it, and he proceeded to run for the touchdown in one of the more miraculous plays that I've ever witnessed as a coach."

The call was known as "Lonesome" because the entire offense is told to run the play as if the ball will be handed off to the running back, when actually the quarterback would be keeping it on a naked bootleg.

Tice recalled it being used in practice to punish the defensive ends for over committing inside and not containing the edge.

"Curt Phillips is smiling and shaking his head like, "Oh yeah, here it comes!" Tice laughed. "So I was like, alright, here we go. I ran it and I came around the corner and I thought, *'I'm going to get smoked.'*"

Two Indiana defenders were in his general area ready to pounce on him, but Tice made the most of the opportunity.

With some blocking assistance from offensive lineman Ryan Groy and backup tight end Rob Korslin, the third-string quarterback flew off his feet and into the end zone.

It would be his first and only collegiate touchdown.

"I didn't know he had that much athleticism in his body when he made that juke and was able to scamper in," Zeitler admitted with a laugh.

"He proved all of us wrong," Chryst admitted. "For those players on the field, that is their opportunity, so you didn't want to handcuff them completely. I certainly didn't think he'd score a touchdown. You're happy for him. It was fun."

Teammates celebrated with Tice not just on the field but the day after in the film room. Most of the quarterback meetings would happen right when a good chunk of those Sunday NFL afternoon games would be on. The back-up would have his cell phone handy, since his father was coaching for the Chicago Bears at the time and Chryst allowed him to check the scores to see how his dad's team was performing.

Chryst, knowing this, asked Tice for a peculiar request.

"'Play *Chariots of Fire*,'" Tice remembered Chryst saying. "We're watching my touchdown run, and the song starts playing – and he put the play in slow-motion. We were just laughing hysterically."

The current Wisconsin head coach was known for dissecting each play in great detail. For Tice's score, it was a one and done.

"We watched it once, and he just said 'Nice work, Ticer,' and that was it. Thankfully, we moved on."

CHAPTER ELEVEN

Next Man Up

One of the finest defensive performances in Wisconsin football history took place during the 2015 Holiday Bowl in San Diego. A combination of expert play-calling and a hungry, amped up linebacker with fresh legs equaled trouble for the USC Trojans.

Trailing 20-14 in the third quarter, the USC had a short field to work with after holding UW to a punt.

Enter inside linebacker Jack Cichy.

Cichy had been bouncing off the walls of the locker room during the first half. Due to a targeting penalty in Wisconsin's 34-24 victory at Minnesota on November 24, the Somerset, Wis. product was forced to sit out the first half of the bowl game.

With USC looking to cut into the Wisconsin lead defensive coordinator Dave Aranda would call three straight blitzes that involved the determined inside linebacker.

Cichy blitzed through the offensive line on the first two sacks and dropped quarterback Cody Kessler each time. On the third blitz, he blew up freshman running back Ronald Jones, hunted down Kessler again and buried him for a seven-yard loss.

From a once promising 1st-and-10 start at midfield the Trojans would have to punt from their own 22 on 4th-and-38.

"I lucked out – I got good play calls," Cichy declared. "They blitzed me every time. The red sea parted on two of them, and I had a little bit of resistance on the last one. I was in the right place at the right time."

Wisconsin would lose the lead early in the fourth quarter, but quarterback Joel Stave led a drive that was capped off by a Rafael Gaglianone field goal – giving UW a two-point advantage with under two-and-a-half minutes left in the game.

Jack Cichy (48) with one of his three sacks of USC quarterback Cody Kessler (6). | AP Photo

Cichy would answer again, pressuring Kessler into throwing an errant pass intercepted by cornerback Sojourn Shelton late in the game. The defense would survive one last onslaught from the Trojans' offense, but would ultimately seal Wisconsin's 23-21 win at Qualcomm Stadium that evening.

Despite only playing 30 minutes on the field, Cichy racked up nine tackles, three sacks, and was named the game's most valuable defensive player. That night, "Cich" earned a new nickname – "Three-Sack Jack."

"That just shows how he played football," fellow linebacker Joe Schobert said. "He's smart. He timed up those blitzes. He's relentless getting after the quarterback. He's at that point in the game, the defense obviously gets hyped when that's going on, and USC had no answer for him on that drive."

It was a coming out party in front of a national audience for Cichy, who finished the year with 60 tackles and five sacks.

Cichy didn't start until the Rutgers game and only after starter Chris Orr went down with a leg injury. Knowing the true freshman Orr wouldn't be able to compete that week, Cichy was willing to move from outside to inside linebacker to help out.

After volunteering to make the move inside in Aranda's 3-4 defense, Cichy had to adjust quickly to a new set of responsibilities.

"On the outside it's pretty easy; you're outside the line of scrimmage, and that's about it," Cichy noted. "T.J. Edwards helped me a lot. Once I figured out my alignments, it's basically just play. You know what's coming from film study."

After settling in against the Scarlet Knights, he finished with eight tackles on the rainy afternoon. It was an indication of things to come as Cichy would go on to have double-digit stops against Maryland and Northwestern. Then came the road game at Minnesota, where he finished with three stops before being flagged on the targeting call that would suspend him for the first two quarters of the Holiday Bowl.

Cichy comes from quite the athletic family. His father was a two-year starter at Notre Dame; his mother was a Marquette basketball player, and sister, Tessa, initially walked on to the Wisconsin women's basketball team. Jack didn't get much notice from Division I schools and was all set to commit to Holy Cross in Massachusetts in January 2013.

That was until then-safeties coach Bill Busch rekindled discussions about joining the program as a walk-on. After visiting Madison, a place where his two sisters attended, he committed to play for UW.

Cichy didn't participate in fall camp until a week and a half into it due to space on the 105-man roster, but he made an impact early on as a member of the punt return and kickoff teams. He officially was recorded as playing in four games that season, making his debut in week two and recording a tackle against Tennessee Tech.

He would redshirt his true sophomore season in 2014, giving him an extra year of seasoning to develop. That decision would significantly help Cichy heading into this third year. His "relentless" attitude on the field, which he admitted may have got him in trouble at times last season, showed up in a huge way in the final two quarters of the season.

"I kind of blacked out because I was out of breath," Cichy recalled of the three-sack sequence. "I remember walking to the sideline and just panting and trying to catch my breath. I was going as fast as I could back-to-back-to-back. It was an unreal feeling."

****

The Holiday Bowl was also a fitting end to the careers of Schobert, wide receiver Alex Erickson, and quarterback Joel Stave, three walk-ons who rose from relative obscurity to contribute heavily throughout their time at Wisconsin.

Walk-ons have stepped in when opportunities have presented themselves at UW. The 2015 season was no different under first-year head coach Paul Chryst.

What stood out was how much of an impact those unheralded players made. It's a rarity to have an offense's leading passer (Stave), rusher (Dare Ogunbowale) and receiver (Erickson) be former walk-ons.

"Where would this team be without the walk-ons?" Erickson asked. "You look at three of the four captains. Joe's the linebacker of the year in the Big Ten. Joel's tied for the all-time wins at Wisconsin. You have Dare stepping in at running back when Corey (Clement) went down. Troy Fumagalli at tight end, Drew Meyer as starting punter, and then Cichy stepping up. Walk-ons made serious impacts on both sides of the ball and special teams."

Meyer quietly played 54 games in his Wisconsin career, tying for the school record with Ethan Hemer and six other players. He also holds the school mark for both single-season and career punts (80 and 256, respectively), statistics the Hartland Arrowhead athlete didn't foresee happening when initially committing to UW.

"I definitely didn't think about career records coming in, although maybe I should have after my freshman year when we punted 80 times that season," Meyer laughed. "When I was recruited, there was a chance I could be a four-year starter, so you obviously have dreams and goals, but it was never an objective to have the most punts – because that means we're not scoring a lot. But it was a huge honor to be in that position and to be a Badger all those years."

Meyer replaced current NFL punter Brad Nortman in 2012 as a redshirt freshman, and went on to average 41.5 yards per kick. He wouldn't average higher than 40 yards per punt the rest of his career, having to adjust to different types of punting schemes with the changes to the coaching staff.

"You take for granted that you have a guy who knows what he's doing, that hits the ball hard and puts it where they want it to go," BadgerBlitz.com's John Veldhuis said. "I think that's what the Badgers look for and what you see out of walk-ons that make the most out of their time. They're consistent, they know what's expected of them, and they're going to work their hardest. I think that's what Drew brought to the table."

****

Like Cichy, Ogunbowale got his chance to shine after stepping in for an injured starter. The Milwaukee native filled in admirably for Corey Clement who missed all but four games in 2015 due to a sports hernia. Ogunbowale led the team in rushing with 819 yards and seven touchdowns.

Though Wisconsin's rushing attack wasn't the traditional rushing attack seen in year's past, Ogunbowale displayed a penchant for pass blocking and catching the ball out of the backfield. He finished second on the team with 36 receptions and provided Stave with another option in the passing game while wide receiver Robert Wheelwright and tight end Austin Traylor were sidelined for extended periods of time.

"Once Corey couldn't go -- it's the next man up," Cichy stated. "It's a great mentality to have, and Dare's done it very well."

Cichy and Ogunbowale share a common bond – they were both awarded scholarships.

During a summer team meeting before the 2015 season, Chryst surprised both with the scholarship announcement. The scene was something Ogunbowale only experienced before as a bystander, congratulating other walk-ons that were awarded for their hard work.

"I wanted to say it was a sigh of relief because I felt like I deserved it, but it was just pure joy," said Ogunbowale with a huge smile.

A year prior to the Holiday Bowl, Ogunbowale was still wrapping his head around how to *be a running back* after transitioning from cornerback. During preparation for Bowling Green in mid-September, head coach Gary Andersen approached Ogunbowale about a position change. A redshirt sophomore at the time, the cornerback had dug in as a back-up behind Shelton and Darius Hillary.

He displayed an elusiveness in space against defenders during drills that popped out to the coaching staff. With depth at running back a concern behind Melvin Gordon and Clement, the pitch was made.

"He was such a good special teams player, he was such a hard worker, and whatever you asked him to do, he wanted

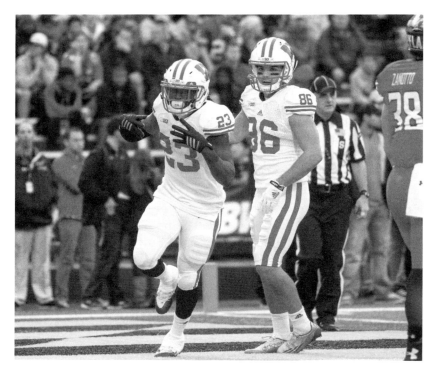

Dare Ogunbowale (23) led UW with 819 yards and 7 touchdowns during the 2015 season. | AP Photo

to be involved," Andersen remembered. "I think it's imperative as coaches we continue to look and see what's best for the kid and where they fit to make the team better, but also to make it better for the young man that's involved in the football program. With Dare, that's the way it was."

"At first, I was like, 'What are you talking about?'" Ogunbowale conceded with a laugh and a grin. "After about 15 seconds thinking about it, I thought there has to be a reason why. He obviously saw something. I jumped on it right away."

What better way to acclimate to a new position than to be thrust into game action right away? Ogunbowale found himself in the backfield near the end of the third quarter, with UW up by 52 against Bowling Green. Three players,

Gordon, Clement and Tanner McEvoy (who was still playing quarterback at the time), would leave the game after each rushing for over 100 yards.

His first carry was a power run to the left, where typically the right guard pulls from the backside to lead the ball carrier. The novice running back took the handoff, and as he described it, the play was beautifully blocked.

"I could have had a touchdown on my first carry of my college career, but I slipped," Ogunbowale said. "That play gave me the confidence though."

The run went for seven yards and set the stage for a big afternoon, gaining 94 yards on 14 carries in the 68-17 blowout. It could have been taken as a grain of salt in mop-up time against an inferior MAC opponent. But with only a handful of practices in the books, and with that shiftiness, maybe this would actually work out?

"He accepted the transition with open arms. He kind of shocked us how far along he was as we went through practice," Andersen explained. "We put him in what we call "inside drill" and then some scout team stuff, and he moved right through it. Then you get into team reps and, all of a sudden, he can do a good job there, too. Then obviously the success he had in the games. I was so proud of him last year to see how he was highly involved and successful in the offense."

As a senior in high school, Ogunbowale watched Wisconsin football from a distance. He had no offers to play football after playing consistently for two years at Marquette High School. He also came to the realization he didn't want to pursue soccer and basketball at the next level. The athletic recruit was content that within a few weeks he'd make his way 90 miles west to Madison as a student.

"Then Coach Strickland calls in August, so fall camp's going on," explained Ogunbowale, who noted his high school head coach, Jeff Mazuczak, had established a rapport with Strickland. "At the time there's that 'The Camp' video series, so I was watching (and thought), 'Ah that'd be awesome if I was on the team.'"

So rather than watch "The Camp," highlighting the football team during its summer camp, Dare now had the opportunity to actually be in it, as an opening in the 105-man roster needed to be filled. He jumped on the opportunity immediately.

That season on the scout team would be a struggle for the all-conference defensive back, though. He stood across the line of scrimmage from a dynamic route runner in Abbrederis on a daily basis. Ogunbowale would continue to grind while developing his body for the college game, crediting strength and conditioning assistant coach Jamil Walker for further improving his physique and mentality in the weight room.

He'd contribute mostly on special teams in 2013 and 2014, continuing to evolve from a physical standpoint as a running back over the course of the season under the tutelage of running backs coach Thomas Brown. After Brown left the program, Ogunbowale would develop further in the mental aspect of the position from returning assistant John Settle.

Ogunbowale picked up Chryst's offense quickly, and also understood how to block potential blitzers on passing downs. Along with his ability in space to make defenders miss as a receiving target out of the backfield, Ogunbowale would be utilized heavily heading into the season.

The amount of carries and on-the-field exposure grew exponentially after Clement suffered the sports hernia injury. Thrust into action as an every down player with less than a year in the backfield, Ogunbowale ran behind an inexperienced offensive line.

Despite some growing pains and injuries on that offensive front, Ogunbowale ran for over 100 yards three times that season – 112 vs Miami (Ohio), 117 at Nebraska, and a career-high 155 yards on 33 carries at Minnesota.

"It was a big season for the walk-ons," Ogunbowale said "We joke about it because obviously we're not walk-ons anymore, but it's funny just looking back at where we were when we first got here. Erickson and I ran down the field on scout kickoff team … Cichy was on scout defense. I remember all of that."

****

Of the entire group, Erickson's journey to Wisconsin might be the most unconventional, which led to confusion about his eligibility back in 2014.

The Darlington, Wis. native enrolled at UW late in the fall of 2011 after deciding not to play basketball at Division III UW-Stevens Point. He joined the team in spring 2012 after Chryst and now-offensive coordinator Joe Rudolph left for Pitt.

Though he combined for 94 total touchdowns in his career as a dual-threat quarterback at Darlington High School, Erickson moved to wide receiver. It's a position he's still working to perfect, though he had some wise mentors ahead of him that guided him in his progression.

"I've only been playing it for four years, so I'm still learning a lot every day," Erickson acknowledged. "You look at it like, 'Oh, running routes can't be that hard' and then you get out there. It's tough because you have to control your body so much, keep your arms moving and keep your feet under you. There's so much to learn about just the route running alone. Then reading coverages, blocking schemes and where you have to go. There was a lot to learn, but I had Jeff Duckworth and Jared Abbrederis, guys that were experienced and played a lot of football here. They knew the positions and the schemes very well."

Though still raw, the former *Wisconsin State Journal* Small School Player of the Year would make his break for playing time beginning in spring 2013. He played in all 13 games with three starts. He caught nine passes on the season, but a nasty hit in the Capital One Bowl against South Carolina tore his meniscus to end his year.

Though the injury wouldn't allow him to finish the bowl game, the snaps he gained provided more confidence moving forward.

"That season I grew so much mentally, more so than just experience on the field," Erickson said. "It was getting over that mental bridge of, 'I can play at this level. I can compete against these guys. I can compete against the best teams in the Big Ten, the best teams in the country.'"

With Abbrederis moving on to the NFL in 2014, there was a need for someone to step up in the receiving corps. Erickson established himself as the No. 1 target for both McEvoy and later Stave.

He reeled in 55 receptions for 772 yards, including a five-catch, 160-yard performance against the Gophers in late November. Fighting through injuries, inconsistent play, and a run-heavy offense with Gordon and Clement – the rest of the position group only caught 39 passes combined.

With Chryst's pro-style offense back in 2015, the wide receivers improved, catching 149 of the 252 team completions. Erickson paced the squad with 77 catches, the second-highest total for receptions in a season behind Abbrederis.

Alex Erickson (86) makes one of his 77 catches during the 2015 season. | AP Photo

Erickson's presence solidified a unit critical to the offense's success during his time in Madison.

"I remember watching him right away when he got here," Stave said of Erickson, who was named UW's offensive player of the year by the coaches with his 973 yards receiving. "I was talking with (former graduate assistant) Luke Swan in Alex's first camp, and just the way he caught the ball, just the way he ran. I thought he was going to end up being a pretty good player. We were dead-on with that. He's very natural. He catches the ball really well with his hands. He's smart, so he's an easy guy to throw to because you know he'll be in the right spot."

****

Erickson would be one of two Badgers honored with first-team All-Big Ten selections in 2015. Both were former walk-ons. While Erickson was a first-team selection by the media, Joe Schobert was a consensus pick and named the conference's linebacker of the year.

Another overlooked in-state product, the Waukesha native finished tied for second in the conference in tackles for loss (19.5), tied for fourth (9.5) in sacks, and led the team with five forced fumbles. He was awarded team MVP honors at the end of the season.

On a national level, Schobert earned first-team All-American honors by the Football Writers Association of America (FWAA) and ESPN, a second-team pick by the AP, CBS and the *Sporting News*. He was a semifinalist for the Chuck Bednarik Award, given to the nation's top defensive player.

Schobert's performance in the Outback Bowl following his junior year is one Badger fans won't soon forget. He recorded six tackles with three tackles for loss, but where he made his mark in Wisconsin's 34-31 victory over Auburn was what he did in overtime.

After Gaglianone put Wisconsin ahead with a 25-yard field goal, Schobert delivered tackles on three consecutive plays, including sniffing out and stuffing an option pass on the Tigers' third down attempt. The ensuing Auburn 45-yard field goal attempt hit off the right upright giving UW the win.

The former walk-on started all 14 games in 2014 and placed fourth on the team in tackles (69), third in tackles for loss (13.5) and led the team in pass breakups (seven) and quarterback hits (five). Though he combined with Vince Biegel to form one of the nation's best outside linebacking duos, he too was passed over by many programs before finding his way to UW.

Like Doering, Schobert was noticed after the annual in-state all-star game. His recruiting courtship with Wisconsin started a month before he was slated to head to North Dakota as a walk-on. The first-team all-state selection was a dangerous running back at Waukesha West, who as a junior broke John Clay's prep record for single-game rushing yards in a state title game. He still went largely unnoticed.

Jed Kennedy, who coached former Badgers running back Melvin Gordon at Kenosha Bradford, was the coach of the WFCA all-star team that year. Kennedy had a familiarity with Schobert from when Waukesha West and Kenosha Bradford squared off in the state semi-final game in 2010. Schobert's role was to keep Gordon and the rest of Bradford's potent offense – which averaged over 50 points a game – from making big plays. Kennedy noted Schobert possessed enough athletic ability and skill to contain the backs. West went onto win 30-15.

In addition to the normal practice routines, Coach Kennedy added in some competitions to liven things up at the all-star game. The south squad featured a number of talented athletes, including some who were Division I scholarship recipients.

"Every time I turned around he was making plays, whether it was on offense, defense, or special teams," Kennedy recalled. "We had a dunk contest on the crossbar, 40-yard dash competition and throwing football event. Joe won them all, outperforming many kids who had offers from UW."

Joe Schobert (58) was named the 2015 Big Ten linebacker of the year. | AP Photo

Coach Kennedy, having developed a relationship with Bielema through Gordon's recruiting process, felt confident that Joe was a talent the Badgers may need to re-evaluate.

"At that point, I knew Joe was something special," Kennedy said, who currently coaches at Brookfield Central. "You just don't see those things out of a high school kid. I had a great relationship with Coach Bielema and felt comfortable making that call."

Bielema contacted Schobert about the preferred walk-on opportunity, but he'd have to move quickly on his application, which he didn't finish due to the perceived lack of interest he received from UW. He filled the application out and sent it in, but didn't hear anything back from the university's admissions office. Time was ticking. A day before he was set to leave for Grand Forks, Bielema called and notified Schobert that he was "100 percent sure" that he would be admitted and able to enroll in fall classes.

Schobert decided to take a shot and join Wisconsin as a preferred walk-on. The coaching staff put him with the wide receivers the first three days of practice, then moved him to safety. Thanks to his work in the weight room, Schobert soon shot up to around 220 pounds and eventually was moved to linebacker. An opportunity on special teams allowed him to see the field in eight games that 2012 season.

"It wasn't like how I envisioned college and pro football players growing up," Schobert said about his jump to big-time college football. "There weren't a bunch of track stars or super humans. I felt like I was one of the guys and fit in pretty well athletically."

Then came the defensive shift to the 3-4 under Andersen and Aranda in 2012. He learned his craft from those veterans in front of him like Brendan Kelly, Armstrong, and Borland. With Armstrong out for the spring, Schobert would receive more reps in helping him further learn the new defensive schemes. He worked his way into the two deep at outside linebacker with Biegel, eventually playing in all 13 games with one start.

Flash forward two years, as Schobert was looking to improve upon his statistically solid junior season. Before the season, however, social media blew up with a feat of his athleticism. During summer conditioning, a round-robin basketball tournament was set up by the strength and conditioning staff for the players. According to Schobert, the players were waiting for the official seedings for the tournament when some of his teammates started attempting to dunk.

With his teammates watching, Schobert drove towards the hoop and slammed home a left-handed windmill dunk. Wide receiver Jazz Peavy caught the post-slam hysteria and posted it on social media. Badgers fans across the nation would take notice of the feat.

One former Badger who took notice was Jim Leonhard, who years earlier won a similar dunk competition.

"He's pushing me," Leonhard said about Schobert's dunk. "It's good to see another walk-on continue the tradition."

"I had a good day of jumping," Schobert said modestly.

Schobert started the 2015 season off with a bang. Though UW lost 35-17 to eventual national-champion Alabama in the opener, he flashed against the Crimson Tide's offensive line. He recorded a couple of sacks and led the team in tackles (13) and tackles for loss (4) that evening in Dallas.

He continued his torrent pace in the conference opener at home against Iowa, entering the contest tied for the national lead in tackles for loss and fourth in sacks. Schobert harassed quarterback C.J. Beathard all afternoon, nearly willing his team to win. He would end the game with eight tackles, five quarterback hurries, 3.5 tackles for loss, three sacks and two forced fumbles. The Badgers lost 10-6, but Schobert's efforts earned him Big Ten co-defensive player of the week.

Schobert capped his senior season off by leading the nation's top scoring defense as UW allowed only 13.7 points per game. Schobert would also tie for 11th in the nation in tackles for loss, averaging 1.5 per game.

More important to Schobert than his impressive statistics was the fact he and Erickson were named two of the four team captains by their peers prior to the season.

"Obviously it's a huge responsibility. It's a big deal to be a captain at the University of Wisconsin," Schobert said. "Every day I'd walk by the list of walk-ons who earned letters, who earned scholarships; the walk-ons who were team captains and played in the NFL. They have all of those lists right outside of the locker room. I looked at that every day and thought, 'I want to get on all of those lists.'"

****

Along with Schobert, Erickson and senior safety Michael Caputo, the fourth captain of that 2015 team was quarterback Joel Stave. Arguably the most polarizing student-athlete the program has ever seen, Stave would leave UW as the winningest quarterback in school history.

Many pundits have noted this particular statistic as a skewed measurement of a quarterback's success (example: Trent Dilfer and the 2000 Baltimore Ravens). At Wisconsin, that argument could be magnified a huge extent as UW's physical running game was the centerpiece of the offense. During Stave's time in Madison, he had the luxury of handing the ball off to NFL-caliber running backs Montee Ball, James White and Melvin Gordon. They ran behind NFL-caliber offensive linemen like Travis Frederick, Rick Wagner and Rob Havenstein.

Everyone agrees football is a team sport, but consider the following facts when assessing the 2015 Wisconsin offense: its usual batch of reliable, homegrown, athletic offensive linemen started seven different combinations in their 13 games, including four redshirt freshmen. With Corey Clement lost for three-quarters of the season, the Badgers could muster only 150.3 yards per contest rushing – good for 94th in the country. Someone else had to step up.

For the first time since Stave's redshirt year, the passing game jumped above 200 yards per contest in 2015. UW threw for 228.3 yards per game, its best mark since 2011.

Change was apparent in the first game against Alabama. One play in the second quarter demonstrated a new assertiveness by the senior signal caller. With under two minutes to go in the first half and Wisconsin driving at Alabama's 39-yard line, Stave threw a pass into the middle of the field where, at first, it appeared no Badgers receiver was. Seconds later, Erickson made his "break" in the route and caught the pass for a huge 23-yard gain. It was a promising development in the UW quarterback's game.

"I think Joel realized he needed to be a difference maker in that game," said Budmayr, who returned to Wisconsin as a graduate assistant working with the offense starting in 2015. "Once he had that confidence and believed in himself, he played differently. You have to give guys around you a chance to make a play. I think that's one area that he grew quite a bit in his senior season – especially with the struggles he went through the year before."

"I had never been good at throwing the ball to a spot and trusting my receivers to get there, and that's what Coach Chryst talked a lot about in practices," added Stave, who finished 26-of-39 for 228 yards in the 2015 season opener. "If it's picked off or incomplete, it's not a big deal, it's practice. You can find out how early you can release the ball and where the receiver is going to be. When you play with that faith in the guys around you, it becomes so much more fun."

Stave ended his career 18-of-27 for 217 yards and a touchdown against USC in the Holiday Bowl. The win – his 31st – would catapult him above Brooks Bollinger for career wins as a starter.

Joel Stave (2) set a UW record with 31 career wins as a starter. | AP Photo

"It means a lot to me," Stave acknowledged. "It was a really cool record to get, and to be able to do it the way we did against a very quality opponent in USC in a bowl game, it was a good way to go out. It was always a goal just to get an opportunity to play as much as I could, because you only have four years of eligibility, and after my redshirt year, I knew my clock was ticking. If I wasn't playing, I was missing opportunities that I wouldn't get back."

His opportunity would come in 2012. Stave started the season as a backup to Maryland graduate transfer Danny O'Brien. In the third game of the season against Utah State, Stave would relieve the former ACC Freshman of the Year at halftime with Wisconsin down 14-3. With the offense stalling, the decision was made to go with Stave. He only completed 2-of-6 passes on the evening, but helped lead the drive ending with Ball's go-ahead touchdown. The Badgers survived 16-14.

Stave would make his first start against UTEP the following week, and his big arm was on display – establishing a walk-on to walk-on connection with Abbrederis on two big passes, including a 47-yard bomb that would be the first of 48 career touchdown tosses. He would finish the game 12-of-17 for 210 yards.

He started six games that season before a broken collarbone against Michigan State forced him out for the rest of the regular season. He displayed promise on the field as he threw six touchdowns compared to three interceptions. More importantly, he kept defenses honest with the threat of a deep pass off of play-action that complimented the three-headed rushing attack of Ball, White and Gordon.

Stave encountered another quarterback competition when Andersen was hired as head coach. This time he would have to fight off Curt Phillips and newcomer Tanner McEvoy, a JUCO transfer who was envisioned by many fans as the future of Wisconsin signal callers. He was a dual-threat player who could beat defenses with his feet as well as his arm. Stave could throw the deep ball, but would never be mistaken for a rushing threat. After a back-and-forth battle during the preseason, the former walk-on retained the starting job for the 2013 season.

Statistically speaking, it was a solid season for Stave, throwing 22 touchdown passes and completing almost 62 percent of his throws. Those 22 touchdown passes are still the second most in a single season in school history. His critics pointed to the errant passes and bad decisions that resulted in 13 interceptions.

McEvoy moved back to quarterback from safety and had a chance to learn the offense during spring practices in 2014. The two battled for the starting position throughout fall camp for the right to start the season against LSU. There didn't seem to be any indication the challenger would dethrone the starter, but according to Stave and offensive coordinator Andy Ludwig, the decision was announced during a meeting a week to 10 days before the opener.

"I thought I was going to be the starter coming out of camp," Stave said. "I thought I deserved to be but then again, that's the game. Every coach wants something different in their offense and their quarterback. I wasn't really thrilled about it, but that's just the way things go sometimes."

"Joel handled it like a total pro," Ludwig remembered. "That was a very difficult conversation. It always is when you've gotta tell one guy he's the man, and the other's the back-up. Joel handled it just the way you would anticipate him to with his chest out, chin up and ready to work to get his job back. I appreciated that very much."

Ludwig remembered a warm and humid practice inside the McClain Center a couple of days after the decision where the footballs were wet and Stave couldn't throw the ball as well as he had before. It may have been the conditions, but something happened, something that the 6-foot-5 Stave – even with his even-keeled personality – couldn't put a finger on.

"I really don't know," Stave conceded in April 2016. "It was frustration for sure. I wasn't real thrilled with some of the decisions that were made, and I let that affect my mood. When it affects your mood, it can really bring you down in multiple aspects. I was kind of disappointed and frustrated and letting it affect me more than I should."

His throwing mechanics were affected. Some have called it "the yips," similar to when a second baseman in baseball can't throw the ball to first base. Others called it a mental block. Either way, he couldn't throw a football the way he used to.

Stave wouldn't play a down in the 28-24 loss against LSU. It was a disappointing defeat, given Wisconsin allowed 21 unanswered points after building a 17-point lead through the third quarter. McEvoy completed only 8-of-24 passes for 50 yards and threw two interceptions. The following Tuesday, the issue with Joel was brought to light to the media, though Andersen tried to protect the former starting quarterback.

"Joel has been dealing with some issues with his throwing shoulder for the last couple of weeks and we have come to a decision, after talking with Joel, that the best thing for him right now is to shut it down and give him some rest," Andersen stated in a September 2 release by the Wisconsin athletic department. "It was a tough decision because Joel is a great competitor and has a tremendous desire to help this team. We will continue to monitor his progress but we're not putting a timetable on his return at this time."

For Stave, however, that didn't sit well, and he agreed to speak to the media. Andersen, stuck in a compromised position in trying to help his quarterback, verbally retracted the statement sent out to the media. Stave didn't have to admit to a dozen media personnel what was going on, but he wanted to set the record straight after discussing the matter with his mom.

"I figured just don't put it out there that I'm having issues with my shoulder," Stave said, "because that can lead to problems down the road where people think I have shoulder problems. I just figured I'd address things and get it out of the way and start moving forward."

"I remember he struggled to get the words out," Potrykus recalled of the interview. "He struggled to adequately explain what he was going through, and I remember feeling so bad for this kid having to basically bare his soul in front of everybody and say, 'I can't throw a football right now, and I can't figure out why.'"

It may have been rock bottom, but Stave wasn't going to let this setback pin him down in defeat. He received support from his teammates, playing catch with those willing to stay after practice to get that "right" feeling back. He also worked with the scout team to help the first-team defense prepare for their upcoming opponents. Most importantly, he started having fun with football again. He started feeling back to his normal self.

"He always stayed positive," Schobert said of Stave, who became close friends with their lockers right next to each other. "When he wasn't starting in 2014, he came down and was throwing for the defense on the scout team so we would get the best look possible until he got back to the starting rotation."

Stave would re-emerge in a game situation against Northwestern on October 4. McEvoy was 4-of-10 for only 24 yards with an interception. With 56 seconds left in the second quarter and UW trailing 10-0, Stave stepped back on the field. It wasn't the prettiest of debuts, as the Greenfield native completed only 8-of-19 passes for 119 yards and three interceptions in a 20-14 loss. Though it wasn't the Hollywood-scripted return he had hoped for, Stave went 8-1 the rest of the season as the starter leading UW to the inaugural Big Ten West Division title.

"He overcame obstacles that you and I can't even come close to appreciating," Ludwig declared. "He didn't exactly know what was going on with him, but he battled and fought his way through it. We couldn't have done it without him."

Stave started 2015 off like a completely new quarterback from years' past. In the first four games, he threw seven touchdown passes to only two interceptions, completing over 66 percent of his passes. Trusting his receivers, and himself, appeared to pay off.

Like all quarterbacks, though, Stave had his bad days. The divisional match-up against Iowa paled in comparison to his first four games of 2015. Stave fumbled twice and threw two more interceptions in a 10-6 loss. A late turnover allowed UW to take over in Iowa territory. Stave, however, tripped on the foot of guard Micah Kapoi and fumbled on the one-yard line. The Hawkeyes recovered, and held on for the win.

Fans always clamor for the next in line, and back-up quarterbacks may be their favorite players on the team. Stave faced criticism, at times rightfully so, as eight of the 44 games he played in he threw multiple interceptions. Looking back, the embattled quarterback knows the public's perception of him is mixed, but he was always honed in on the objectives at hand during the season.

"It doesn't feel good when stuff is written or said about you, but if I just avoided it, it's almost like ignorance is bliss," Stave explained. "As long as it was not in the forefront of my mind, it didn't bother me. I knew it was out there, and I knew people weren't saying the most positive things about me. But I knew how my teammates felt about me, I knew how my coaches felt about me, and that's really all that mattered. I kept everything else blocked out and focused on myself, the team and school."

"I think Joel had a consistent approach, but I think that he learned how to deal with the criticism through the course of his career," Chryst added. "We're all human. I appreciate how he handled everything and thought he was really good. It's a process, and we're all shaped by our experiences. I think he focused on the things that were in his control. He was unwavering in his work ethic and his approach. Most of all, he kept faith in himself."

While criticizing some of his onfield play, Badgers fans should also remember Stave for his many solid performances. Under Ludwig and later Chryst, he developed the ability to drive down the field in a hurry-up, up-tempo offense. In the 2015 Outback Bowl, he led the team on its last offensive series with the help of a dominant Gordon. On a crucial 4th-and-5, he completed a seven-yard pass to tight end Sam Arneson to continue the 64-yard drive, which led to the game-tying field goal and forced overtime.

In UW's come-from-behind victory at Nebraska, Stave led the Badgers to points in four of their final five drives. On their last two possessions, he completed 6-of-9 passes for 98 yards. The final series set up Gaglianone's game-winning 46-yard field goal. If not for a controversial, overturned call on Jazz Peavy's touchdown catch against Northwestern on Senior Day, Stave would have redeemed himself of two earlier interceptions. Before the incompletion, he was 5-of-7 for 73 yards, leading the offense down to the NU one-yard line.

Stave ended his collegiate career on a high note earning the Holiday Bowl's offensive player of the game honors. He also cemented his place in school history. Not only does he own the all-time wins record, he also holds the single-season record for pass attempts and completions (370 and 225, respectively, in 2015) and both the career and single-season record for 200-yard games (18 and nine). He has the third-best winning percentage for quarterbacks (.756), and is second all-time in career passing yards (7,635), passing attempts (1,031) and completions (613).

Stave was named the 2014 Comeback Player of the Year. He was also honored with the Tom Wiesner Award in 2015, following a line of eight former walk-ons who had previously received the award. He was a captain, and he was a winner. Despite the calls for his ousting from a portion of the fan base, Stave kept a calm tone and kept striving, kept driving – something he's done his whole career.

"Fans are fans. They're living and dying with their teams. I know how painful the lows can be for fans sometimes," Stave said with a laugh. "I appreciate the support. Criticism comes with the position. You look at any quarterback in America, there's always going to be a handful of people talking about how bad they are. Until you get to be Tom Brady or someone like that, people aren't going to be real thrilled with their quarterback. I understand that it's the nature of the position."

CHAPTER TWELVE

The Legacy Comes Full Circle

The 2016 schedule for the Wisconsin Badgers may just be the most difficult in modern school history. UW takes on highly-touted LSU, now with former UW defensive coordinator Dave Aranda, to start the season in Lambeau Field on September 3. A daunting slate of conference match-ups begins in the fourth week of the season, starting with road match-ups against Michigan State and Michigan, then a bye week to prepare for Ohio State on October 15. UW heads back on the road to Iowa City to face the Hawkeyes, fresh off their Rose Bowl appearance followed by a Saturday evening bout with interdivision foe Nebraska.

Wisconsin fans who have thrown fits about an apparently weak conference schedule in recent years shouldn't have anything to complain about.

Gone are the four captains from 2015. The Cleveland Browns selected Schobert with the 99th overall pick in the 2016 NFL Draft, and he was recently named the starter at outside linebacker for them. Stave and Erickson signed free agent deals with the Minnesota Vikings and Cincinnati Bengals, respectively. Erickson made the Bengals final roster, while Stave is on the Vikings practice squad.

The walk-ons may not be depended upon as heavily as they have been in previous seasons, but over a handful could make an immediate impact in different phases of the game in 2016.

One such player is Joe Ferguson. Ferguson has racked up 24 tackles through three years at Wisconsin, including starting a game back in 2014 against South Florida. He's primarily been utilized as a special teams player who may see more time at safety in the two seasons he has left in Madison.

He's also Barry Alvarez' grandson.

It's one of those fun endings to a story where everything comes full circle. Coach comes to downtrodden football program, establishes a walk-on tradition that's helped lift a team to championships, only to have his grandson be a part of that tradition.

The first-team all-conference and all-region quarterback from Madison Memorial High School almost didn't come to UW.

"Wisconsin was always talking to me," Ferguson said. "I basically grew up in their backyard, and they always kept tabs on me and knew me because of the family connection, but I really wanted to explore all of my options. At the end of the day, none of the other schools really worked out. UW was the one school that was giving me the opportunity to play football. I could have gone to a Division II or Division III program, but I wasn't interested in that. Like everyone else, I was interested in playing at the highest level even though a lot of people didn't think that I could. I felt that I could, and my family thought I could."

Ferguson is in line to contribute like fellow walk-on safeties Doering, Leonhard, Stellmacher, Hampton and Maragos, who made their mark early on special teams and earned substantial time on the field.

"He doesn't want people thinking he's going to be treated differently because he's my grandson," Alvarez noted. "He wants to be his own guy. I respect that."

Alvarez makes sure to keep his distance and let Ferguson make his own name while in Madison, though he did consult

Joe for his thoughts on a particular coaching matter.

After Gary Andersen bolted to Oregon State following the Big Ten Championship game in 2014, Alvarez was asked by the team's seniors to lead the program into their January 1 bowl game. Before accepting, he wanted the opinion of his grandson.

"'Let me think about it, and I'll call you in the morning,'" Alvarez recalled telling the seniors. "So I called Joe on my way home that night and told him the seniors wanted me to coach the team and asked what he thought about it."

When he heard the news, Ferguson was all for it.

"When he finally asked me if he should coach, I said, 'Absolutely. Look at all of the people in this program and how they respect you. It would be tremendous for you to come and coach and show them a different mentality,'" Ferguson said.

So grandfather would coach grandson, and UW's 34-31 bowl game victory would serve as the stepping stone into the Paul Chryst era.

Former walk-on and Badger great, Jim Leonhard, has come full circle returning to coach the secondary at UW. Here he is seen with head coach Paul Chryst and new defensive coordinator, Justin Wilcox. | AP Photo

For Ferguson there would be one more surprise. Secondary coach Daronte Jones would leave Madison in February for a position with the NFL's Miami Dolphins.

On February 21, a homecoming of epic proportions took place in Madison. The new secondary coach would be none other than Alvarez' former prized walk-on Jimmy Leonhard.

How fitting a return is it that not just a former walk-on, but *the* epitome of the walk-on tradition would come back to Wisconsin?

"I've been thinking about Jimmy, and we've had conversations," Chryst acknowledged. "Certainly when Daronte had the opportunity to go to Miami, I was excited for him to do what's best for him. When talking with Jimmy, the question was always if something like this was presented, would he be interested?"

Given the chance of returning to the program was undoubtedly intriguing, but Leonhard weighed whether or not to take the job. Having just finished up a decade playing in the NFL and having a year off to spend time with his family allowed him to feel, as he put it, spoiled. Being a stay-at-home dad would forge strong bonds within his young family. On top of that, though lauded for his ability to be a coach on the field during his playing days, Leonhard had never formally coached at the collegiate or professional level.

"It was the same mentality of coming here as a walk-on. I would have been kicking myself if I didn't take that opportunity," Leonhard explained. "I think I would have felt the same way if I didn't take the opportunity to coach, especially here at my alma mater, the only place I really want to coach right now. If I would have passed it up, I would have had that in my head. If it's a long-term job or not, I'm going to figure that out over the next couple of years, but it was a step I needed to take to have peace of mind with where I'm at in my career."

If anyone could jump straight into coaching, it would be Leonhard. Just months into his time at UW, the all-time leader in interceptions has started to shape his secondary in preparation of facing a high-powered LSU team. It's been a transition, one he knew would be coming after contemplating his next step in life prior to joining Wisconsin.

"Obviously it has been a complete flip as far as being very busy as a coach and not being home nearly as much. It has been an adjustment. I've loved every second of the coaching side as far as being with the guys and building those relationships and building the trust within the group," Leonhard said. "That's the part of the game I love. I haven't been on the coaching side of football with the recruiting, the scheduling, the time management. I've done it as a player, but it's just a little bit different as a coach. But it's been a blast so far."

The irony of having the former walk-on back on the staff at Wisconsin – looking to uncover the next great walk-on – is not lost on Chryst.

"One of the neat things to me is that the story is not done being written," Chryst said regarding the tradition of the walk-on program. "It's on-going. The legacy is that it's an integral part of the program. Everyone comes to us in a different path. The thing I'm proud of is that it didn't matter how you got here, it's what you did when you were here. What you did was celebrated, appreciated and valued."

BIBLIOGRAPHY

The authors conducted over 100 original interviews with former and current players, coaches and media for this book. They would like to thank all for their time and contributions, as well as acknowledge those authors and journalists whose original writings helped clarify stories.

Books

Alvarez, Barry and Mike Lucas. *Don't Flinch - Barry Alvarez: The Autobiography The Story of Wisconsin's All-Time Winningest Coach.* KCI Sports Publishing: 2006.

Dawidoff, Nicholas. *Collision Low Crossers: Inside the Turbulent World of NFL Football.* Back Bay Books: 2014.

Doherty, Justin and Brian Lucas. *Tales from the Wisconsin Badgers Sideline: A Collection of the Greatest Badgers Stories Ever Told.* Sports Publishing: 2012

Kennedy, Chris. *No Bed of Roses: My Sideline View of the Badgers' Return to Greatness.* Trails Books: 2007

Lepay, Matt. *Why Not Wisconsin? From Barry to Bo: Broadcasting the Badgers from the Best Seat in the House.* Triumph Books. 2012.

Newspapers
The Capital 2008
Capital Times 1990-94, 1998-2008
Colorado Springs Gazette 2012
The Eau Claire Leader-Telegram 1993
Greensburg Daily News 1994
The Herald Bulletin 2001
The Intelligencer Record 1994, 2000
Kenosha News 1992-93
Milwaukee Journal
Milwaukee Journal Sentinel 1996-97, 2007
Milwaukee Sentinel 1993
Racine Journal Times 1993
Wisconsin State Journal 1990-2016
The Tribune-Democrat 1999

Other Media
Wisconsin Football Media Guides: 1990-2007
2015 Wisconsin Badgers Football Fact Book
Box scores and game summaries (PDF) from
UWBadgers.com

Websites
Abcnews.com
Aseaofblue.com
Badgerherald.com
BadgerofHonor.com
BaltimoreRavens.com
BaltimoreSun.com
Blog.Chron.com
Buckys5thQuarter.com
Campusrush.com
Chicagotribune.com
Cleveland.com

ClevelandBrowns.com
Collegespun.com
Courant.com
CUBuffs.com
DailyCardinal.com
Dailyunion.com
ESPN.com
ESPNWisconsin.com
Fox6Now.com
FoxSports.com
Gazettextra.com
Grantland.com
GreenfieldNow.com
HoustonChronicle.com
HoustonTexans.com
Isthmus.com
Journaltimes.com
JSOnline.com
LakeCountryNow.com
LATimes.com
Lubbockonline.com
LukeSwan.com
Madison.com
MensHealth.com
Milehighreport.com
Mlive.com
NCAA.org
NFL.com
NYDailyNews.com
Omaha.com
Onwisconsin.uwalumni.com
OregonLive.com
Packers.com
Patriotsdaily.com

Philly.com

Post-gazette.com

Profootballfocus.com

Profootballtalk.nbcsports.com

Scout.com sptimes.com

Suntimeshighschoolsports.com

Theplay-book.com

Thepresstribune.com

UCFKnights.com

UCLABruins.com

UWBadgers.com

Walterfootball.com

WAOW.com

Wiscnews.com

Wisconsin.rivals.com

Wissports.net

WKOW.com

WALK-ON LETTERWINNERS

Tyler Adam
Jeffrey Wirth
Chris Hein
Matt Krueger
Joe Panos
Sam Veit
Vince Zullo
Todd Anthony
Jason Levine
Chad Cascadden
Phillip Chavez
Chris Kennedy
John Rhymes
Rick Schnetzky
Robert Nelson
Scott Young
Steve Baffico
Bryan Jones
Steve Kouba
Dave Anderson
Bob Adamov
Michael Brin
Troy Hegg
Greg Keigher
Eric Pollex
Dan Schneck
Demetrius Brown
Eric Grams
Trent Gross
Mike Schneck
Eric Skrzypchak

Dirk Stanger
Joe Steffen
Donnel Thompson
Scott Wagner
Matt Davenport
Mark Davis
Jason Doering
Joe Innis
Eric Mahlik
Ben McCormick
Mike Solwold
Mark Tauscher
Delta Triplett
Jason Eck
Pat Gill
Kevin Kampmann
Matt Unertl
Erik Waisanen
Erik Bickerstaff
David Braun
Mark Downing
Philip Koch
Jason Schick
Chuck Smith
Bret Burlingame
Josh Hunt
Russ Kuhns
Nick Mueller
Ryan Simmons
Chris Wagner
Mike Allen

Nick Cochart
Pat Ellestad
Matt Katula
Jim Leonhard
Jesse Mayfield
Matt Mialik
R.J. Morse
Kirk Munden
Mark Neuser
Stephon Watson
Nate Howard
Kyle McCorison
Jason Clemens
Matt Gajda
Zach Hampton
Fred Nieforth
Joe Stellmacher
Ken DeBauche
Paul Hubbard
Ben Strickland
T.J. Wielebski
Casey Hogan
Steve Johnson
Victor Meckstroth
Josh Neal
Joel Nellis
Bill Rentmeester
Dywon Rowan
Luke Swan
Josh Balts
Matt Brown
Nate Egholm
Tyler Holland
Jeff Holzbauer
Derek Konkol
Mike Van Someren
Derek Yentz

Ryan Flasch
Will Hartmann
Ben Landgraf
Brian McCulliss
Erik Prather
Joe Sibley
Paul Standring
Bradie Ewing
Chris Maragos
Robert Burge
Nate Emanuel
Matt Groff
Adam Hampton
Jordan Hein
Richard Kirtley
Rob Korslin
Andrew Lukasko
Tony Megna
Chukwuma Offor
Rick Wagner
J.J. Watt
Kyle Wojta
Drew Woodward
Jared Abbrederis
Ethan Armstrong
Ethan Hemer
James McGuire
Kyle Zuleger
Coddye Ring-Noonan
Alec Lerner
Nick Hill
Jerry Ponio
Nate Tice
Connor Cummins
Kyle French
Greg Russo
Brock DeCicco

Jacob Ninneman
Joel Stave
Marcus Trotter
Trent Delinger
Brett Arnold
Lance Baretz
Alex Erickson
Drew Meyer
Jerry Ponio
Derek Straus
Joe Schobert
Chris Gill
Ben Ruechel
Jack Russell

Connor Udelhoven
Dare Ogunbowale
Andrew Endicott
Joe Ferguson
Troy Fumagalli
Logan Schmidt
Thad Armstrong
Evan Bondoc
Jack Cichy
Ryan Connelly
Zander Neuville
P.J. Rosowski
Ryan Wickesberg

WALK-ONS WHO EARNED SCHOLARSHIPS

Tyler Adam
Jeffrey Wirth
Chris Hein
Joe Panos
Sam Veit
Vince Zullo
Chad Cascadden
Robert Nelson
Scott Young
Steve Baffico
Dave Anderson
Bob Adamov
Michael Brin
Eric Pollex
Dan Schneck
Dirk Stanger

Donnel Thompson
Scott Wagner
Matt Davenport
Jason Doering
Joe Innis
Ben McCormick
Josh Dickerson
Eric Mahlik
Mike Solwold
Mark Tauscher
Jason Eck
Matt Unertl
David Braun
Mark Downing
Jason Schick
Chuck Smith

Bret Burlingame
Ryan Simmons
Mike Allen
Nick Cochart
Jim Leonhard
Kirk Munden
Matt Gajda
Zach Hampton
Joe Stellmacher
Ken DeBauche
Paul Hubbard
Ben Strickland
Casey Hogan
Steve Johnson
Josh Neal
Joel Nellis
Bill Rentmeester
Dywon Rowan
Luke Swan
Tyler Holland
Will Hartmann
Erik Prather
Bradie Ewing
Chris Maragos
Robert Burge
Nate Emanuel
Jordan Hein
Richard Kirtley

Rob Korslin
Rick Wagner
J.J.Watt
Kyle Wojta
Kyle French
Jared Abbrederis
Ethan Armstrong
Ethan Hemer
Kyle Zuleger
Brock DeCicco
Joel Stave
Marcus Trotter
Drew Meyer
Joe Schobert
Lance Baretz
Trent Denlinger
Alex Erickson
Joe Ferguson
Troy Fumagalli
James McGuire
Ben Ruechel
Connor Udelhoven
Jack Cichy
Ryan Connelly
Andrew Endicott
Zander Neuville
Dare Ogunbowale
Ryan Ramczyk

WALK-ON CAPTAINS

Joe Panos (1993)
Bob Adamov (1998)
Donnel Thompson (1998-99)
Jason Doering (1999-2000)
Jim Leonhard (2003-04)
Ken DeBauche (2007)
Ben Strickland (2007)
Luke Swan (2007)
Chris Maragos (2009)
Bradie Ewing (2011)
Rick Wagner (2012)
Alex Erickson (2015)
Joe Schobert (2015)
Joel Stave (2015)
Dare Ogunbowale (2016)

WALK-ONS IN THE NFL

Joe Panos
Chad Cascadden
Mike Schneck
Mark Tauscher
Donnel Thompson
Michael Solwold
Erik Bickerstaff
Jason Doering
Matt Katula
Jim Leonhard
Paul Hubbard
Chris Maragos
J.J. Watt
Bradie Ewing
Rick Wagner
Jared Abbrederis
Alex Erickson
Joe Schobert